Musical Feasts

DETROIT SYMPHONY ORCHESTRA

Musical Feasts

DETROIT SYMPHONY ORCHESTRA

Dedication

To our friends and colleagues, the superb musicians of the Detroit Symphony Orchestra,
whose artistic excellence and unselfish and enthusiastic participation in our projects
continually inspire and enrich our lives.

Detroit Symphony Orchestra Volunteer Council

Musical Feasts

A Cookbook by the Detroit Symphony Orchestra Volunteer Council

Copyright© 2001 by
Detroit Symphony Orchestra, Inc.
3663 Woodward Avenue, Suite 100
Detroit, Michigan 48201-2444
313-576-5100

This cookbook is a collection of favorite recipes,
which are not necessarily original recipes.

Library of Congress Catalog Number: 2001 135010
ISBN: 0-9710550-0-9

Edited, Designed, and Manufactured by
Favorite Recipes® Press
An imprint of

FRP

P.O. Box 305142
Nashville, Tennessee 37230
800-358-0560

Art Director: Steve Newman
Book Design: The Eleazar Group
Project Manager: Linda A. Jones

Manufactured in the United States of America
First Printing: 2001
10,000 copies

Acknowledgements

We wish to acknowledge everyone who contributed
to the production of this cookbook. We thank them for
their assistance, advice, and support.

Edward Deeb, President, Michigan Food and Beverage Association
Sylvia Rector, Food Editor, *Detroit Free Press*

Photography
Detroit Free Press: J. Kyle Keener, Chief Photographer, *Detroit Free Press*
Detroit Symphony Orchestra Archives

Non-recipe Text
Detroit Symphony Orchestra Publications
Recollections of Musicians: Felix Resnick,
Paul Ganson, Ervin Monroe, Douglas Cornelson,
Robert Williams, Donald Baker

DSO Administrative Assistance:
Susan Burns, Marilou Carlin, Chuck Dyer,
Virginia Fallis, Mami Kato, Mark Rulison, Sally Baker,
Tiffany Stozicki, Anne Wilczak, Jill Woodward

Committee

Cookbook Committee Chair: Jean Carman

Recipe Compiling and Testing:
Jean Azar, Mary Beattie, Gwen Bowlby, Carol Bozadzis,
Gloria Clark, Millie Everson, Susan Giffin, Barbara Goodwin,
Paulette Groen, Helen and Gus Kokas, Mary Ellen Miller,
Gloria and Stan Nycek, Fay Ann Resnick, Andrea Rogers,
Patricia Senecoff, Jennifer Shandler, Julie Stackpoole,
Eloise Tholen, Aynne Zazas

Marketing:
Mary Beattie, Gwen Bowlby, Lynne Dewey, Barbara Goodwin,
Ann Lawson, Sue Nine, Carol Skruch, Julie Stackpoole, Joan Stern

Table of Contents

Preface

ozart wrote his greatest divertimenti as dinner music. Fine food and great music are a combination that appeals to all our senses. This cookbook is the outgrowth of just such a combination of food and music. Musical Feasts has been a popular fund-raiser for many years for the Detroit Symphony Orchestra Volunteer Council. Its growing success and popularity inspired this collection of recipes, many of which were served at Feasts.

The annual series of Feasts involves loyal supporters of the Orchestra opening their homes, hosting brunches, luncheons, formal dinners, and barbecues. An important part of each event is a musical program performed by members of the Detroit Symphony Orchestra. Guests have a unique opportunity to enjoy good food and great music in an intimate setting while getting to know these wonderful individuals, our musicians.

The recipes offered in this book are favorites from the kitchens of noted chefs, musicians, visiting artists, friends of the Orchestra, and members of the Volunteer Council. Recipes are never entirely new, but often are variations of old favorites, and no claim is made that these are all original. We hope you also enjoy reading some of our *Musical Feasts* menus, and perhaps find an idea for your own special occasion. Thank you for helping us support our Detroit Symphony Orchestra with your purchase of *Musical Feasts*.

The Musical Feasts *Cookbook Committee*

Detroit Symphony Orchestra

Founded in 1914, the Detroit Symphony Orchestra is heard live by more than 450,000 people annually in a year-round performance schedule that includes twenty-six weeks of Classical subscription concerts, as well as a DTE Energy Pops Series, Ameritech Paradise Jazz Series, Holiday Festival, *The Detroit News* Young People's Concerts, and a diverse summer season.

A leader in music education since its founding, the DSO has education/outreach activities that include free annual concerts, presented at Orchestra Hall, for 32,000 Detroit and metro-area schoolchildren. Additional programs include concerts featuring the DSO's training ensembles, the Detroit Symphony Civic Orchestra, and Civic Sinfonia; the Summer Institute at Meadow Brook, a two-week music camp for students; the In A Chord program, which brings musicians into classrooms; a Fellowship program for African-American musicians; and the African-American Composers Residency.

Continuing its long broadcast tradition, the DSO is currently the most listened-to orchestra in the United States. Its classical concerts are recorded live at Detroit's historic Orchestra Hall and broadcast nationally on General Motors "Mark of Excellence" radio series. Hosted by one of America's most famous radio and television personalities, Dick Cavett, the broadcasts are heard by over one million listeners each week on nearly five hundred radio stations across the country.

Over the years, the Orchestra has amassed a long and distinguished recording catalog with albums on the Victor, London, Decca, Mercury, RCA, Chandos, and DSO labels. During Paul Paray's tenure as music director (1951–62), the DSO made over sixty-five recordings on the Mercury label, many of which are still highly sought-after in reissues. Music Director Antal Dorati's (1977–81) DSO recording of Stravinsky's *The Rite of Spring* was the first CD to win the prestigious Grand Prix du Disque Award, Europe's highest honor. Since 1990, Music Director Neeme Järvi and the Orchestra have released over thirty compact discs. Their first release, containing American music, was critically acclaimed and appeared on *Billboard* magazine's Top Classical Album chart for fourteen weeks.

Throughout its history, the Orchestra has toured extensively, both nationally and internationally. This includes three highly acclaimed European tours: in 1979, performing in twenty-four cities; in 1989, appearing in fourteen music capitals; and in 1998, touring eight countries and sixteen cities, including Maestro Järvi's hometown, Tallinn, Estonia. In November 1998, the DSO traveled to the Far East for the first time, where it performed eight concerts in Toyota City and Otsu City, Japan.

In 1996, the DSO announced a three-phase plan for the Orchestra Place Development Project, an educational, performing arts, and office/retail complex on eight acres of land surrounding Orchestra Hall. Phase I, now complete, is a five-story office building and eight-hundred-car parking structure.

The next phase is the Max M. Fisher Center for the Performing Arts, which will include new patron amenities and a second performance hall. Anchoring this expansion will be the new

Jacob Bernard Pincus Music Education Center, which will provide music learning programs for people of all ages. The new facilities are slated to open in the fall of 2003.

The final phase is a new Detroit High School for the Performing Arts and Communication and Technology Center to open in the fall of 2004.

Preludes

Brunch
&
Appetizers

Brunch

Brunch

Artichoke Brunch Casserole

8   ounces sliced fresh mushrooms
1   tablespoon butter
2   (10-ounce) packages frozen artichoke hearts,
        cooked, drained
2   cups chopped cooked ham
8   hard-cooked eggs, quartered
1   (10-ounce) can cream of mushroom soup
1   tablespoon chopped onion
1/4   cup sherry
1   bay leaf
1/2   teaspoon salt
1/4   teaspoon garlic salt
    Curry powder to taste
3/4   cup shredded Swiss cheese or Cheddar cheese

Sauté the mushrooms in the butter in a skillet until tender. Layer the artichoke hearts, ham, hard-cooked eggs and sautéed mushrooms in a buttered baking dish. Mix the soup, onion, wine, bay leaf, salt, garlic salt and curry powder in a bowl. Pour over the layers. Sprinkle with the cheese. Bake at 400 degrees for 25 minutes. Discard the bay leaf before serving.

Serves 6 to 8

Christmas Brunch

2   cups soft bread cubes (about 3 or 4 bread slices)
1   cup milk
8   eggs
2   tablespoons butter
8   slices bacon, cooked, crumbled
8   ounces Swiss cheese, shredded
1/2   teaspoon seasoned salt
1/2   cup fine bread crumbs
1   teaspoon butter

Mix the bread cubes and milk in a large bowl. Let stand until the milk is absorbed. Scramble the eggs in 2 tablespoons butter in a skillet. Add to the bread cube mixture and mix well. Stir in the bacon, Swiss cheese and seasoned salt. Spoon into a greased 8×8-inch baking pan. Brown the bread crumbs in 1 teaspoon butter in a skillet. Sprinkle over the top. Chill, covered, for 8 to 12 hours. Bake, uncovered, at 400 degrees for 15 minutes.

Serves 6

Note: This recipe is good warm or cold. You may double the recipe and bake in a 9×13-inch baking pan.

Twenty-Four Hour Wine and Cheese Omelets

A great do-ahead breakfast omelet.

1	*large loaf dry French or Italian bread, broken into small pieces*
6	*tablespoons unsalted butter, melted*
12	*ounces Swiss cheese, shredded*
8	*ounces Monterey Jack cheese, shredded*
9	*thin slices Genoa salami, coarsely chopped*
16	*eggs*
3¼	*cups milk*
½	*cup dry white wine*
4	*large green onions, minced*
1	*tablespoon Düsseldorf German mustard*
¼	*teaspoon freshly ground black pepper*
⅛	*teaspoon ground red pepper*
1½	*cups sour cream*
⅔	*to 1 cup freshly grated Parmesan cheese or shredded Asiago cheese*

Arrange the bread in 2 buttered 9×13-inch baking dishes. Drizzle with the melted butter. Sprinkle with the Swiss cheese, Monterey Jack cheese and salami. Beat the eggs, milk and wine in a mixing bowl until foamy. Stir in the green onions, mustard, black pepper and red pepper. Pour over the layers in each dish. Chill, covered with foil, for 8 to 12 hours.

Remove from the refrigerator about 30 minutes before baking. Bake, covered, at 325 degrees for 1 hour or until set. Remove the foil. Spread the sour cream over the top of each omelet. Sprinkle with the Parmesan cheese. Bake, uncovered, for 10 minutes or until the top is crusty and light brown.

Serves 12

Weston Gales
Detroit Symphony Orchestra
Director
(1914–1917)

Many great institutions have sprung from small beginnings. In 1914, ten young women contributed one hundred dollars apiece and pledged to find one hundred subscribers to donate ten dollars each to start a community orchestra in Detroit. They brought in Weston Gales, a young church organist from Boston, who had conducted concerts in Europe, to be the orchestra's director. The first concert was held February 26, 1914. The concert was greeted with enthusiasm, and the newspapers predicted a great future. If they could see the cultural jewel and important civic institution that is the Detroit Symphony Orchestra of today, they would be amazed and very proud. From 1914 to the present, the Orchestra has weathered many ups and downs, from depressions to world wars, to take its place as a dynamic presence on the music stage of the world. Looking to the future and building on the past, the Detroit Symphony Orchestra is a leader in bringing classical music education, performance, and appreciation to everyone in its listening range.

Brunch

Sausage Strudel

2 pounds bulk sausage
2 pounds mushrooms, chopped
1 medium onion, chopped
   Butter
16 ounces cream cheese, softened
1 (17-ounce) package puff pastry

Brown the sausage in a large skillet, stirring until crumbly; drain. Sauté the mushrooms and onion in a small amount of butter in a skillet until tender. Add to the sausage and mix well. Stir in the cream cheese. Unfold the puff pastry sheets. Divide the sausage mixture between the 2 puff pastry sheets, spreading to the edges. Roll up as for a jelly roll, tucking the ends under. Arrange seam side down on a baking sheet. Bake at 400 degrees for 20 minutes.

Serves 4 to 6

Note: You may wrap the Sausage Strudel before baking and freeze for later use. To serve, unwrap and bake at 450 degrees for 10 minutes. Reduce the oven temperature to 400 degrees. Bake for 1 hour longer.

Fontina, Asparagus and Leek Strata

1 tablespoon butter or margarine
5 cups 1-inch slices asparagus (about 1 1/2 pounds)
2 cups thinly sliced leeks (about 3 small)
1/2 cup water
3 tablespoons chopped fresh parsley
2 teaspoons minced fresh tarragon, or 1/2 teaspoon dried tarragon
1 teaspoon grated lemon zest
1/4 teaspoon salt
1/8 teaspoon pepper
12 (1-ounce) thin slices firm white sandwich bread
1 cup shredded fontina cheese
2 1/2 cups 1% low-fat milk
3 eggs
1 egg white
1/8 teaspoon pepper
1 1/2 cups fresh bread crumbs (about 3 slices)

Melt the butter in a large nonstick skillet over medium-high heat. Add the asparagus, leeks and water. Bring to a boil. Cover and reduce the heat. Simmer for 10 minutes or until tender, stirring occasionally. Stir in the parsley, tarragon, lemon zest, salt and 1/8 teaspoon pepper. Layer the bread, asparagus mixture and cheese 1/2 at a time in a 9×13-inch baking dish coated with nonstick cooking spray. Beat the milk, eggs, egg white and 1/8 teaspoon pepper with a whisk in a bowl until blended. Pour over the layers. Chill, covered, for 8 to 12 hours. Uncover the strata and sprinkle with the bread crumbs. Bake at 400 degrees for 40 minutes or until set.

Serves 6

Joe's Texas Breakfast

4   *flour tortillas*
1   *cup frozen O'Brien potatoes*
2   *tablespoons butter*
2   *eggs*
2   *tablespoons milk*
1¹/2   *cups tortilla chips, crumbled*
6   *to 8 thin slices Cheddar cheese or Monterey Jack cheese*
¹/4   *cup salsa*

Wrap the tortillas in foil. Bake at 250 degrees until warm. Sauté the potatoes in the butter in a skillet until softened and warm. Beat the eggs and milk in a bowl. Pour over the potatoes. Sprinkle with the crumbled tortilla chips. Cook until the eggs are soft-cooked, stirring constantly with a spatula. Turn off the heat.

Arrange the cheese slices over the egg mixture. Cover and let stand for 3 minutes or until the cheese melts. Remove the flour tortillas from the oven and unwrap. Place ¹/4 of the egg and cheese mixture at 1 end of each tortilla. Top each with 1 tablespoon salsa and roll up.

Serves 4

Ossip Gabrilowitsch
Detroit Symphony Orchestra
Director
(1918–1936)

Ossip Gabrilowitsch, who attended the Leningrad Conservatory, was an internationally known pianist whose presence gave the DSO instant credibility. He inspired the construction of Orchestra Hall after saying he would accept the position of Music Director if the Orchestra had a proper hall. He contributed $5,000 himself, and the community instantly rallied. Built in just four months and twenty-three days, the new Hall opened for its first season October 23, 1919. Gabrilowitsch was able to bring some of the most prominent musicians of the day to Detroit, including Rachmaninoff, Stravinsky, Enrico Caruso, and Marian Anderson. In 1922, with Artur Schnabel as guest pianist, he led the Orchestra in the world's first radio broadcast of a symphonic concert on WWJ-FM. Later, in the 1930s, the Orchestra was heard regularly on the Ford Sunday Evening Hour. When he died in 1936, Gabrilowitsch left an impressive record of accomplishment during his long tenure at one of America's acoustical marvels.

B r u n c h

Crème Brûlée French Toast

1/2   cup (1 stick) unsalted butter
1   cup packed brown sugar
2   tablespoons corn syrup
1   loaf challah, French or rustic Italian bread
5   eggs
1 1/2 cups half-and-half
1   teaspoon vanilla extract
1   teaspoon Grand Marnier
1/4   teaspoon salt

Heat the butter, brown sugar and corn syrup in a saucepan until the butter melts and the mixture is smooth, stirring constantly. Pour into a 9×13-inch baking dish. Cut the bread into 1-inch slices. Trim the crust from each slice. Arrange the bread in the prepared baking dish, cutting some of the bread into pieces so the entire bottom surface of the dish is covered. Beat the eggs, half-and-half, vanilla, Grand Marnier and salt in a bowl using a whisk. Pour over the bread. Chill, covered, for 8 to 12 hours. Uncover and bring to room temperature. Bake at 350 degrees on the middle oven rack for 40 minutes or until puffed and the edges are golden brown.

Serves 4 to 6

Out-of-This-World Waffles

2 1/2 cups flour
1/4   cup baking powder
1 1/2 tablespoons sugar
3/4   teaspoon salt
2 1/2 cups milk
3/4   cup vegetable oil
2   eggs
1   teaspoon vanilla extract

Mix the flour, baking powder, sugar and salt in a bowl. Add the milk, oil, eggs and vanilla and mix well. Pour the batter into the center of a hot waffle iron. Cook using the manufacturer's instructions.

Serves 6 to 8

Fruit Compote

1   (1-pound) package pitted prunes
8   ounces dried apricots
1   (8-ounce) can mandarin oranges
1   (13-ounce) can juice-pack pineapple chunks
1   (22-ounce) can cherry pie filling
1/2   to 2/3 cup sherry

Combine the prunes, apricots, undrained mandarin oranges, undrained pineapple, pie filling and sherry in a large bowl and mix well. Pour into a 2 1/2-quart baking dish. Bake, uncovered, at 350 degrees for 1 hour.

Serves 8

Almond Scones with Devonshire Cream

This recipe was served at the 1999 Musical Feast Tea and History, hosted by Phyllis Strome.

Almond Scones

2	cups baking mix (Bisquick)
1	tablespoon (heaping) sugar
1	tablespoon sliced almonds or to taste
1	egg
2/3	cup heavy cream
	Few drops of almond or vanilla extract
1	egg white
	Sugar to taste

Devonshire Cream

2	cups whipping cream
1/2	cup confectioners' sugar
1	cup sour cream

For the scones, mix the baking mix, 1 tablespoon sugar and almonds in a large bowl. Add the egg, cream and almond extract and mix well. Shape into 1- to 1 1/2-inch-thick domes. Arrange on a baking sheet sprayed with nonstick cooking spray. Brush with the egg white. Sprinkle with sugar. Bake at 425 degrees for 12 minutes.

For the cream, beat the whipping cream in a mixing bowl until soft peaks form. Add the confectioners' sugar gradually, beating until stiff peaks form. Fold in the sour cream.

Serve the scones with the cream and jam or lemon curd.

Serves 16

Note: You may substitute currants, raisins, chocolate chips or other nuts for the almonds.

Paul Paray
Detroit Symphony Orchestra
Director
(1952–1962)

Paul Paray, brought to Detroit from his native France by John B. Ford, proved to be what the Orchestra needed to return to its former stature after difficult financial times. National radio broadcasts were resumed and a full season of concerts was scheduled. The Orchestra returned to the recording studio, and nearly seventy albums were recorded for Mercury Records. Many of these fine records are still sought after today.

Maestro Paray maintained his vigor and health with an unusual routine. He ate barely any food during the day, walked several miles every morning before rehearsal, and consumed a substantial dinner after every concert. His midday meal consisted of several large cloves of garlic, which was quite apparent to the first row of the Orchestra. However, the musicians note, Paul Paray last conducted the Detroit Symphony Orchestra when he was ninety-five years old. They say it must have been the garlic.

B r u n c h

Harland Sanders' Kentucky Biscuits

In 1953 two honeymooners received this recipe from Colonel Sanders at his Bristol, Tennessee/Virginia Restaurant.

1¹/2   cups flour
1   tablespoon baking powder
1   tablespoon salt
1   tablespoon sugar
1   cup (scant) milk
¹/4   cup lard or shortening

Sift the flour, baking powder, salt and sugar into a bowl. Make a well in the center. Add most of the milk and lard to the well in the flour. Begin squeezing the lard and flour gradually into the milk to form a soft dough, adding the remaining milk as needed. Knead on a floured surface until smooth. Cut with a biscuit cutter. Arrange on a baking sheet. Bake at 450 degrees for 12 to 15 minutes or until golden brown.

Makes 13 biscuits

Apple Coffee Cake

6   apples, peeled, cored, sliced
5   tablespoons sugar
5   teaspoons cinnamon
3   cups flour
2   cups sugar
1   tablespoon baking powder
1   teaspoon salt
1   cup vegetable oil
4   eggs
¹/4   cup orange juice
1   tablespoon vanilla extract

Combine the apples, 5 tablespoons sugar and cinnamon in a bowl and toss to coat. Sift the flour, 2 cups sugar, baking powder and salt into a large bowl. Make a well in the center. Add the oil, eggs, orange juice and vanilla. Beat with a wooden spoon until smooth. Spoon ¹/3 of the batter into a greased 9- or 10-inch tube pan. Drain the apple mixture of any excess liquid. Arrange ¹/2 of the apple mixture in a ring on top of the batter, making sure not to touch the side of the pan. Repeat with ¹/2 of the remaining batter and remaining apple mixture. Spread the remaining batter over the top. Bake at 375 degrees for 1¹/4 hours or until the coffee cake tests done, covering with foil if the top begins to overbrown. Cool in the pan until lukewarm. Invert onto a serving plate.

Serves 10

Note: You may substitute sliced fresh peaches for the apples.

Christopher Parkening's Coffee Cake

¹/2   teaspoon baking soda
3   cups buttermilk
6   cups flour
4¹/2   teaspoons baking powder
1¹/2   teaspoons salt
1   tablespoon cinnamon
1¹/2   teaspoons nutmeg
3   cups sugar
3   eggs
1¹/2   cups vegetable oil, or 1¹/2 cups (3 sticks) butter, melted
1¹/2   cups packed brown sugar
2¹/4   teaspoons cinnamon
       Butter

Stir the baking soda into the buttermilk. Let stand for 10 minutes. Sift the flour, baking powder, salt, 1 tablespoon cinnamon and nutmeg into a mixing bowl. Add the sugar, eggs and oil and mix well. Stir in the buttermilk mixture. Pour into 3 greased and floured 9-inch baking pans or 1 greased and floured 9×13-inch baking pan. Sprinkle with a mixture of brown sugar and 2¹/4 teaspoons cinnamon. Dot with butter. Bake at 350 degrees for 30 to 35 minutes or until the coffee cake tests done.

Serves 15

Sixten Ehrling
Detroit Symphony Orchestra
Director
(1963–1973)

Sixten Ehrling, a multitalented Swede, succeeded Paul Paray in 1963. During his tenure, he introduced a wide array of new music to the Orchestra's repertoire and led it through a very ambitious period of music-making. He conducted 722 concerts and presented twenty-four world premieres in the ten years that he led the DSO. During a tour to Worcester, Massachusetts, in the 1960s, Maestro Ehrling was playing bridge with some of the musicians after a concert. Glancing out the window of the tenth-floor room, he saw the five members of the horn section, led by the principal horn player, inching their way along a narrow ledge, laughing all the way. Horrified, Ehrling shouted, "That's my horn section! My **whole** horn section!" Although the players were unhurt and the concert the next night went well, it took Ehrling a while to recover. In 1973, he left to become head of the Orchestral Department of The Juilliard School in New York.

B r u n c h

Wellesley Coffee Cake

Wellesley Coffee Cake is a favorite of many alumnae of the eastern women's college.

2   cups sifted flour
1   teaspoon baking powder
1/4 teaspoon salt
1   cup (2 sticks) butter, softened
2   cups sugar
2   eggs
1   cup sour cream
1/2 teaspoon vanilla extract
1/2 teaspoon almond extract
1   cup chopped pecans
4   teaspoons sugar
1   teaspoon cinnamon

Mix the flour, baking powder and salt in a bowl. Beat the butter and 2 cups sugar in a mixing bowl until light and fluffy. Add the eggs 1 at a time, beating well after each addition. Add the sour cream and flavorings and mix well. Beat in the flour mixture.

Combine the pecans, 4 teaspoons sugar and cinnamon in a bowl. Pour 1/3 of the batter into a greased and floured 10-inch tube pan. Sprinkle with 3/4 of the pecan mixture. Pour in the remaining batter. Sprinkle with the remaining pecan mixture. Bake at 350 degrees for 1 hour.

Serves 16

Note: You may make this coffee cake up to 2 days ahead of serving. This coffee cake also freezes well.

Kiss Me Cake

2   cups flour
1   cup sugar
1   teaspoon baking soda
1   teaspoon salt
1/2 cup milk
2   eggs
1   (6-ounce) can frozen orange juice concentrate, thawed
1/2 cup (1 stick) margarine, softened
1   cup raisins
     Cinnamon-sugar
1/3 cup chopped walnuts (optional)

Combine the flour, sugar, baking soda, salt, milk, eggs, 1/2 cup of the orange juice concentrate, margarine and raisins in a large mixing bowl. Beat at low speed for 30 seconds. Beat at medium speed for 3 minutes. Pour into a greased and floured 9×13-inch cake pan.

Bake at 350 degrees for 40 to 45 minutes or until the cake tests done. Cool in the pan briefly. Drizzle with the remaining orange juice concentrate. Sprinkle with cinnamon-sugar and walnuts.

Serves 15

Holiday Sweet Bread

2   oranges
2   cinnamon sticks
4   whole cloves
4   cups water
2^1/$_2$ cups (5 sticks) butter
1^1/$_2$ cups milk
2^1/$_2$ cups sugar
1   teaspoon mace
1   teaspoon ground cinnamon
     Pinch of nutmeg
^{1}/$_2$ teaspoon salt
5   envelopes dry yeast
4   eggs
14 to 19^1/$_4$ cups bread flour (4 to 5^1/$_2$ pounds)
1   egg, beaten
     Toasted sesame seeds

Squeeze the oranges, reserving ^{1}/$_2$ cup of the juice. Bring the orange peels, cinnamon sticks, cloves and water to a boil in a 3-quart saucepan and reduce the heat. Simmer for 30 minutes. Remove from the heat. Remove the cinnamon sticks, cloves and orange peels and discard. Add the butter, milk and reserved orange juice to the hot liquid and stir until the butter melts.

Mix the sugar, mace, cinnamon, nutmeg, salt and yeast in a large mixing bowl. Add 4 eggs and the milk mixture. Mix well using your hands until the yeast and egg yolks are evenly distributed. Knead in 14 cups flour. Continue adding enough of the remaining flour and kneading until the dough is soft and not sticky. Cover and let rise in a warm place for 2 to 3 hours or until doubled in bulk. Punch down the dough. Cover and let rise for 2 to 3 hours longer. Divide the dough into 5 equal portions on a lightly floured surface. Shape into loaves. Place in 5 lightly floured 5×9-inch loaf pans. Cover and let rise for 1 hour or until doubled in bulk. Brush the loaves with the beaten egg. Sprinkle with toasted sesame seeds. Bake at 350 degrees for 40 to 50 minutes or until dark brown. Invert onto wire racks to cool.

Makes 5 loaves

Antal Dorati
Detroit Symphony Orchestra
Director
(1977–1980)

Antal Dorati was a regal, demanding, Hungarian-born American with an international reputation and a fiery personal style. Under his strong influence, the Orchestra began recording again, with great success. The DSO recording of Stravinsky's *The Rite of Spring* was the first CD to win the *Grand Prix du Disque*, one of Europe's highest honors. Dorati took the DSO on its first European tour in 1979, to great reviews and acclaim. He was a taskmaster and strove for excellence. During one taxing rehearsal, a principal string player said that he was uncomfortable with a passage that he had to play. "If you wanted to be comfortable, my dear," replied Dorati, "you should have gone into the clergy." On another occasion, the orchestra was rehearsing a section that was difficult for one of the woodwind players. After several unsuccessful attempts, he protested, "But Maestro, I'm doing the best I can." "I know," said Dorati, "and that is what worries me."

B r u n c h

Corn Bread Casserole

*Makes a nice accompaniment to serve
with ham for brunch.*

1   (6-ounce) package corn muffin mix
1   egg
1/2 cup milk
3   dashes of Tabasco sauce
1   (15-ounce) can cream-style corn
1/2 cup chopped onion
3   tablespoons butter
1   cup sour cream
1   cup shredded sharp Cheddar cheese

Combine the corn muffin mix, egg, milk, Tabasco
sauce and corn in a large bowl and mix well. Pour into
a greased 9×9-inch baking pan.

Sauté the onion in the butter in a skillet. Spoon over
the corn mixture. Dollop the sour cream over the
sautéed onion. Sprinkle with the Cheddar cheese.
Bake at 425 degrees for 25 to 30 minutes or until
cooked through.

Serves 6 to 8

Note: This recipe may be doubled.

Pumpkin Walnut Bread

3 1/2 cups flour
1   cup packed light brown sugar
1 1/2 tablespoons baking powder
1/2   teaspoon salt
1   teaspoon cinnamon
1/2   teaspoon nutmeg
1   cup canned pumpkin
1/2   cup (1 stick) unsalted butter or margarine,
        softened
2   eggs, beaten
1 1/2 cups chopped toasted walnuts

Sift the flour, brown sugar, baking powder, salt,
cinnamon and nutmeg in a bowl. Beat the pumpkin,
butter and eggs in a large mixing bowl until smooth.
Add the flour mixture and mix well. Fold in the
walnuts. Divide the dough into 2 equal portions. Press
into 2 greased and floured 4×8-inch loaf pans. Bake at
350 degrees for 35 to 40 minutes or until the loaves
test done. Remove from the oven. Invert onto wire
racks to cool.

Makes 2 loaves

Pumpkin Streusel Bread

Streusel Topping

1/4 cup chopped pecans
2 tablespoons sugar
1 1/2 tablespoons butter or margarine, cut into small pieces
1/4 teaspoon cinnamon

Pumpkin Bread

2 cups flour
1/2 cup sugar
1/2 cup raisins
1 teaspoon baking soda
1 teaspoon salt
1/2 teaspoon cinnamon
1/2 teaspoon ground cloves
1/2 teaspoon nutmeg
1 cup canned pumpkin
1/2 cup plain reduced-fat yogurt
1/2 cup honey
1/4 cup vegetable oil
1 teaspoon vanilla extract
2 eggs

For the topping, combine the pecans, sugar, butter and cinnamon in a small bowl and mix well until crumbly.

For the bread, mix the flour, sugar, raisins, baking soda, salt, cinnamon, cloves and nutmeg in a large bowl using a whisk. Make a well in the center. Combine the pumpkin, yogurt, honey, oil, vanilla and eggs in a medium bowl and mix well. Add to the well in the flour mixture and stir just until moistened. Spoon into a 5×9-inch loaf pan sprayed with nonstick cooking spray. Sprinkle with the topping. Bake at 350 degrees for 1 hour or until a wooden pick inserted in the center comes out clean. Cool in the pan on a wire rack for 10 minutes. Remove from the pan and cool completely on a wire rack.

Serves 16

Note: Use a serrated knife to slice the loaf.

Günther Herbig
Detroit Symphony Orchestra
Music Director
(1984–1990)

Highly acclaimed Music Director Günther Herbig continued the tours of the East Coast initiated by Antal Dorati, recorded for RCA, and resumed the DSO's coast-to-coast radio broadcasts. Perhaps his finest hour came in 1989 when, on a European tour of fourteen cities, the Orchestra was roundly praised in all quarters for its sterling performances. Although Günther Herbig left the DSO in 1990, the Herbigs maintain their home in the Detroit area and Maestro Herbig is a welcome guest conductor with the Detroit Symphony Orchestra.

Brunch

A Half-Yard French Bread

1   *envelope dry yeast*
1   *tablespoon sugar*
2   *teaspoons salt*
     Dash of ground ginger
1¹/₂ *cups hot water*
4¹/₂ *cups flour*
     Cornmeal
     Hot water for brushing

Combine the yeast, sugar, salt and ginger in a large mixing bowl. Add 1¹/₂ cups hot water and stir just to combine. Let stand until the mixture begins to foam. Add ¹/₂ of the flour and beat until smooth. Add the remaining flour and mix to form a slightly sticky dough. Shape the dough into a ball in the bowl. Cover and let rise in a draft-free place until doubled in bulk.

Grease a large baking sheet lightly and sprinkle with cornmeal. Divide the dough into 2 equal portions on a lightly floured surface. Pat each portion into an 8×12-inch rectangle. Roll each rectangle into a loaf, pinching together as you roll and using your palms to shape the tapered ends. Place the loaves side by side on the prepared baking sheet. Cover and let rise for 45 minutes or until doubled in bulk. Cut 3 shallow slashes in the top of each loaf. Brush generously with hot water. Bake at 425 degrees for 15 minutes. Reduce the oven temperature to 325 degrees. Remove the loaves from the oven. Brush with hot water again. Return to the oven. Bake for 30 minutes or until the loaves sound hollow when tapped on the bottom. Remove to a wire rack. Cool in a drafty place for a crisp crust.

Makes 2 loaves

*Note: You may double the recipe and make
3 larger loaves. This recipe also makes great French
rolls and pizza crusts.*

Butterhorn Rolls

1   *envelope rapid-rise yeast*
¹/₄ *cup warm water*
¹/₂ *cup shortening*
¹/₂ *cup sugar*
¹/₂ *teaspoon salt*
³/₄ *cup milk, scalded*
3   *eggs, lightly beaten*
4   *to 5 cups flour*

Dissolve the yeast in the warm water in a bowl. Cream the shortening and sugar in a large mixing bowl until light and fluffy. Add the salt, scalded milk and yeast mixture and mix well. Beat in the eggs. Add 4 cups flour gradually, beating well after each addition. Knead about 10 times on a lightly floured surface, adding enough of the remaining flour to prevent the dough from being sticky. Place in a lightly greased bowl, turning to coat the surface. Cover and let rise for 1¹/₂ hours or until doubled in bulk.

Punch down the dough. Divide the dough into 3 equal portions. Roll each portion into a circle on a floured pastry cloth. Cut each circle into 12 wedges. Roll each wedge up from the wide end. Arrange on nonstick baking sheets. Cover and let rise until doubled in bulk. Bake, uncovered, at 400 degrees for 7 to 9 minutes or until golden brown.

Makes 3 dozen

Neeme Järvi's Easy Estonian Pancakes

Maestro Järvi likes to fill these with honey and cranberry preserves.

1	cup water
1/2	cup flour
1	egg
1/4	teaspoon salt
1	tablespoon vegetable oil

Process the water, flour, egg, salt and oil at low speed in a blender until smooth. The batter should be thin, but not runny. Heat a greased 8-inch frying pan until very hot. Pour enough batter into the hot pan to coat the entire bottom of the pan. Cook for 1 minute. Turn with a spatula. Cook for 1 minute. Remove to a warm platter. Repeat until all of the batter is used. Spread the pancakes with a filling of your choice and roll up.

Makes 3 pancakes

Neeme Järvi
Detroit Symphony Orchestra
Music Director (1990–present)

The arrival of Neeme Järvi soon after the Detroit Symphony Orchestra returned to Orchestra Hall proved to be the spark needed to once again capture international acclaim. The Estonian-born Järvi's infectious enthusiasm and personal excitement about music of every genre struck a chord with the DSO musicians. Like predecessor Ossip Gabrilowitsch, Järvi attended the Leningrad Conservatory and had extensive experience in Europe before coming to Detroit. The combination of three powerful entities—superb musicians, a charismatic and strong leader, and an acoustically perfect hall—have enhanced the worldwide reputation of the DSO. The proof lies in the increase in concert subscription sales, tours to Europe and Japan, radio broadcasts heard on over five hundred stations nationwide, and more than three dozen highly praised recordings. Widely sought-after as a guest conductor, Järvi has won the praise of international music critics as one of the most inspired conductors of today. At home, the strong bond between Järvi and his musicians is important in producing exciting music, and this music, coupled with his delicious sense of humor, brings Detroit audiences to their feet with cries of "Encore! Encore!"

Appetizers

Calypso Black Bean Hummus

2 cups cooked black beans
1 tablespoon tahini paste
1 tablespoon olive oil
1/2 tablespoon lemon juice
1 tablespoon chopped fresh garlic, or to taste
Pinch of cumin
Pinch of sea salt or kosher salt
Black bean cooking liquid or water

Process the black beans, tahini paste, olive oil, lemon juice, garlic, cumin and sea salt in a food processor until mixed. Add bean liquid or water a small amount at a time to make of the desired consistency, processing constantly. Spoon into a serving bowl. Chill, covered, in the refrigerator. Serve with plantain chips, corn chips or toasted pita bread.

Serves 8 to 10

Jackie's Favorite Salsa

2 cups uncooked black-eyed peas
6 cups hot water
4 beefsteak tomatoes, finely chopped
1/2 onion
2 jalapeños, seeded
Zest and juice of 1 lemon
Zest and juice of 1 lime
Juice of 1 orange
2 tablespoons cumin
1 tablespoon coriander
1 teaspoon cayenne pepper
3 to 4 dashes of Tabasco sauce
2 tablespoons tomato paste
2 tablespoons olive oil (optional)

Cook the black-eyed peas in the hot water in a 2-quart saucepan until tender; drain. Process the tomatoes, onion and chiles in a food processor until ground. Add the lemon zest, lemon juice, lime zest, lime juice and orange juice and process well. Place in a stainless bowl. Add the cumin, coriander, cayenne pepper, Tabasco sauce and tomato paste and mix well. Add the drained black-eyed peas and olive oil and mix well. Chill, covered, for 8 to 12 hours.

Serves 6

Tabouli Appetizer

*This traditional Middle Eastern dish is a favorite
of the DSO musicians.*

1	cup fine cracked wheat
1	bunch green onions, finely chopped
2	large bunches fresh parsley, finely chopped
1/2	bunch fresh mint, finely chopped (optional)
4	large tomatoes, finely chopped
	Juice of 4 lemons
1/2	cup olive oil
	Salt and pepper to taste

Soak the wheat in enough water to cover in a bowl for
a few minutes; drain. Squeeze the wheat dry by
pressing between your palms. Combine the green
onions, parsley, mint and tomatoes in a bowl and mix
well. Add the wheat, lemon juice, olive oil, salt and
pepper and mix well. Serve with fresh lettuce leaves,
grape leaves or Syrian bread used as scoops.

Serves 6

Note: You may also serve this dish as a salad.

Grosse Pointe Grandeur
Grosse Pointe

Enter the elegance of one of Grosse Pointe's grand
old homes and be transported to the charming
ambiance of a Loire Valley chateau.

Saturday, June 27th, 1992
7:00 p.m.

Hosts
Mr. and Mrs. Alfred J. Fisher III

Menu
Onion Puffs
Tabouli (at left) with Pita Bread
Fruit Salad with Poppyseed Dressing
Three Medallions—Veal, Beef, Lamb
Roast Potatoes
Tomato Basket with Asparagus
Chocolate Fantasy

Appropriate Wines and Cocktails

Music
Darryl Jeffers, DSO Violin
Alvin Score, DSO Violin
David Ireland, DSO Viola
John Thurman, DSO Violoncello

Appetizers

Anchovy Tapenade

1   *cup black olives*
¹/₂ *cup anchovies*
¹/₃ *cup capers*
2   *tablespoons ground garlic*
¹/₂ *cup olive oil*
    Dash of pepper

Rinse the olives, anchovies and capers separately in cold water to remove some of the salt; drain. Process the olives, anchovies, capers and garlic in a food processor until puréed. Add the olive oil gradually, processing constantly until incorporated. Season with pepper. Serve with sautéed red bell peppers and French bread.

Makes 3 cups

Party Nut Pâté with Date and Mint Chutney

Party Nut Pâté

2   *cups garlic and herb cream cheese, softened*
3   *cups pecans, toasted, ground*
2   *dashes of Tabasco sauce*
    Fresh bread crumbs
    Finely chopped fresh parsley

Date and Mint Chutney

8   *ounces chopped pitted dates*
¹/₂ *cup chopped white onion*
1   *tablespoon red wine vinegar*
¹/₂ *cup water*
¹/₂ *cup banana nectar*
2   *tablespoons chopped fresh mint*
    Pinch of cayenne pepper
    Pinch of salt and black pepper

For the pâté, combine the cream cheese, pecans and Tabasco sauce in a bowl and mix well. Shape into a 12-inch log. Coat with bread crumbs and parsley. Roll in plastic wrap. Chill until firm.

For the chutney, combine the dates, onion, red wine vinegar and water in a saucepan. Cook, covered, over low heat until the dates are softened and the liquid is absorbed. Stir in the banana nectar, mint, cayenne pepper, salt and black pepper.

To assemble, cut the pâté into slices. Top with the chutney. Garnish with fruit and serve with crackers or pita triangles.

Serves 6

Itzhak Perlman's Very Fattening Chopped Chicken Livers

1   pound chicken fat
1   pound chicken livers
1   medium onion, finely chopped
3   hard-cooked eggs, chopped
    Salt to taste

Dice the chicken fat and place in a heavy saucepan. Add a small amount of water. Heat over low heat until melted. Strain through cheesecloth to remove the brown particles. Return the hot rendered fat to the saucepan. Add the chicken livers and turn off the heat. Stew for 6 minutes. Add the onion. Stew until the onion is light brown and the livers are ready; drain, but not too much. Remove to a large bowl and chop. Stir in the hard-cooked eggs. Season with salt. Spoon into a serving bowl. Serve with matzoh or rye bread.

Serves 8

Note: If you want more tang, add uncooked chopped onions. (That's the way my mother used to make it.) Make sure you have plenty of antacids—but it's worth it!

Itzhak Perlman
Principal Guest Conductor

Itzhak Perlman, world-renowned violinist and Principal Guest Conductor of the Detroit Symphony Orchestra, will lead the DSO in concerts for three weeks each season. In addition to conducting, Perlman will participate in the Orchestra's educational activities, providing students with a valuable experience in learning from one of the most respected figures in classical music. As a connoisseur of fine food and wines, Perlman will be able to sample a wide range of cuisines while enjoying the best of classical music with our Musical Feasts program.

Appetizers

Avocado Dip

2   *avocados, peeled, pitted*
2   *tablespoons sour cream*
2   *garlic cloves, crushed*
2   *tablespoons olive oil*
     Juice of 1 lemon
     Salt to taste

Combine the avocados, sour cream, garlic, olive oil, lemon juice and salt in a mixing bowl and beat until fluffy. Chill, covered, in the refrigerator. Spoon into a serving dish. Serve with chips or crackers.

Serves 6 to 8

Cheesy Mexican Dip

8   *ounces cream cheese, softened*
2   *bunches green onions, chopped*
1   *(4-ounce) can chopped green chiles, drained*
1   *(10-ounce) can chili without beans*
2   *cups shredded Cheddar cheese*

Spread the cream cheese in the bottom of a pie plate or small baking dish. Sprinkle with the green onions and green chiles. Spread the chili carefully over the layers. Sprinkle the cheese evenly over the top. Bake at 350 degrees for 20 to 25 minutes or until heated through and the cheese melts. Serve with tortilla chips or corn chips.

Serves 10

Shrimp Taco Spread

8   *ounces cream cheese, softened*
1/4 *cup heavy cream*
1/2 *(12-ounce) bottle chili sauce*
1   *(4-ounce) can cooked tiny shrimp, drained,*
      rinsed, patted dry
6   *scallions, chopped*
3/4 *cup chopped green bell pepper*
1   *(4-ounce) can pitted black olives, drained,*
      patted dry, sliced
8   *ounces shredded mozzarella cheese*

Beat the cream cheese and cream in a mixing bowl until smooth. Pat in an even layer on a serving platter. Layer the chili sauce, shrimp, scallions, bell pepper, olives and cheese in the order listed over the cream cheese mixture. Chill, covered, for 1 hour or longer before serving. Serve with firm tortilla chips.

Serves 8

Roasted Corn Blini with Trio of Caviar

1   to 1¹/2 cups fresh corn kernels
      Sugar to taste
1   cake compressed yeast
2   cups scalded milk, cooled to 85 degrees
1¹/2 cups sifted flour
1   tablespoon sugar
3   egg yolks
1   tablespoon butter, melted
¹/2 cup sifted flour
1   teaspoon salt
3   egg whites
      Sour cream
      Trio of yellow, red and black caviar

Toss the corn kernels and sugar to taste lightly in a bowl. Pour into a shallow baking pan. Bake at 350 degrees until light golden brown.

Dissolve the yeast in the milk in a large bowl. Stir in 1¹/2 cups flour and 1 tablespoon sugar. Let rise, covered, in a warm place for 1¹/2 hours.

Beat the egg yolks and butter in a bowl until blended. Stir in ¹/2 cup flour and salt. Add to the yeast mixture and beat well. Let rise, covered, for 1¹/2 hours.

Beat the egg whites in a mixing bowl until stiff but not dry peaks form. Fold into the batter. Fold in the roasted corn. Let stand for 10 minutes.

Drop by spoonfuls into a hot lightly greased skillet. Cook over medium heat until light brown on each side, turning once. Keep warm until ready to serve. Serve each with a small dollop of sour cream and a trio of yellow, red and black caviar.

Serves 4

A Mexican Fiesta
Bloomfield Hills

If you are a connoisseur of fine art and sculpture, beautiful architecture, rare editions of classic books and fine food, this is the feast for you. The hosts' library is a treasury of first editions, including the works of Orwell, Sinclair, Henry Miller and Galileo. This evening will provide food for both body and soul.

Sunday, May 7, 2000
6:30 p.m.

Your Hosts
Dr. and Mrs. Stanley H. Levy
Mrs. Barbara Frankel

Menu
Salsa Bruschetta (Fresh and Tangy)
Con Queso Dip with Green Chiles and Spicy Sausage
Roasted Corn Blini with Herb Sour Cream and a
Trio of Caviar (at left)
Mixed Baby Greens with Jicama Slaw, Fresh Goat
Cheese Topped with Orange Vinaigrette
Chimichurri Marinated Rack of Lamb with Fresh Herb
Persillade (page 89) and Natural Lamb Jus
Dauphine Potato
Fresh Baby Vegetables
New York Style Cheesecake with Almond Graham
Cracker Crust, Topped with Chocolate Sauce and
Passion Fruit Purée

Pinot Grigio Wine
Coffee and Tea

Musical Performance
DSO Percussion Ensemble

Appetizers

Warm Crab and Artichoke Dip

¹/4   cup cream cheese, softened
¹/2   cup (about) Hellmann's mayonnaise
     Salt and pepper to taste
³/4   cup canned crab meat, drained
¹/4   cup grated Parmesan cheese
3   tablespoons chopped drained marinated
      artichoke hearts
2   tablespoons sliced green onions
2   tablespoons chopped red bell pepper
2   tablespoons chopped celery
1   tablespoon chopped fresh Italian parsley
1¹/2   teaspoons sherry vinegar
¹/2   teaspoon Tabasco sauce
2   tablespoons grated Parmesan cheese

Beat the cream cheese in a mixing bowl until smooth. Add the mayonnaise and beat well. Season with salt and pepper. Fold in the crab meat, 1/4 cup Parmesan cheese, artichoke hearts, green onions, bell pepper, celery, parsley, vinegar and Tabasco sauce. Spoon into a 2- to 4-cup soufflé dish. Sprinkle with 2 tablespoons Parmesan cheese. Bake at 400 degrees for 15 minutes or until the Parmesan cheese melts. Serve with toasted baguette slices.

Serves 8

Note: For toasted baguette slices, arrange baguette slices on a baking sheet. Bake at 400 degrees for 10 minutes.

Shrimp Mousse

2   envelopes unflavored gelatin
¹/2   cup cold water
8   ounces cream cheese, softened
1   (10-ounce) can tomato soup
1   cup mayonnaise
1   onion, finely chopped
1   cup finely chopped celery
1   cup chopped green olives
1   (4-ounce) can small shrimp, drained
2   slices pimento-stuffed olive

Soften the gelatin in the cold water in a bowl. Heat the cream cheese and tomato soup in a saucepan until the cream cheese melts. Stir in the mayonnaise. Add the gelatin mixture. Heat until the gelatin mixture dissolves, stirring constantly. Stir in the onion, celery, chopped olives and shrimp. Pour into a lightly greased large fish or shrimp mold. Chill until set. Unmold onto a serving platter lined with romaine. Arrange the olive slices on the mold to resemble fish eyes. Serve with assorted crackers.

Serves 12

Seafood Quenelles with Champagne Sauce

Seafood Quenelles

4   *ounces each bay scallops, rock shrimp and lobster tail*
1/2   *teaspoon each paprika and salt*
1/4   *teaspoon white pepper*
4   *ounces heavy cream*

Champagne Sauce

4   *cups fish stock*
1   *cup white wine*
2   *cups heavy cream*
1/2   *teaspoon salt*
1/4   *teaspoon white pepper*

For the quenelles, clean the seafood and drain well. Squeeze out any excess moisture. Purée the seafood in a food processor. Add the paprika, salt and white pepper and mix well. Add the cream gradually, processing constantly until incorporated. Drop by tablespoonfuls in batches of 6 at a time into simmering water in a saucepan. Poach for 4 to 5 minutes or until firm and cooked through. Remove with a slotted spoon to a tray lined with paper towels. Keep warm. Repeat with the remaining batter.

For the sauce, combine the fish stock and wine in a saucepan. Cook until the mixture is reduced to a syrupy consistency. Stir in the cream. Cook until reduced to a mixture thick enough to coat the back of a spoon. Season with salt and white pepper.

Serve the warm quenelles with the sauce.

Serves 10

Cocktails on the River
Grosse Ile

Whisk yourself away to a touch of the Hamptons in Michigan! Bring your blanket and spend an elegant afternoon with us on the spacious lawns situated on one of the most beautiful stretches of the Detroit River. Sit in the meditation garden surrounded by a rippling moat or see your own reflection in the koi-filled pond. The free form pool features sculptures of children appreciating summer vacation; its disappearing edge seems to whisper to the bronzes that summer will never end—a hope you'll share this Sunday afternoon.

Your Hosts
Linda and Michael Starling

Menu
Tri-Colored Pepper Risotto Cakes
Warm Potato Pancakes with a Dollop of Applesauce
Double Tomato Jam
Spicy Cashew Chicken on Wonton Crisps with
Sesame Seed Garnish
Sliced Tenderloin of Beef with a Variety of
Mini Buns and Sauce Béarnaise
Mediterranean Cheese and
Garlic-Stuffed Portobello Mushrooms
Seafood Quenelles (at left) with Lobster Sauce
Blackened Pearls of Swordfish with Red Currant Coulis
Smoked Salmon with Traditional Garnishments
Char-Grilled Strips of Chicken and Bow Tie Pasta
in a Creamy Garlic Dressing
Haricots Vert Wild Mushroom Salad in
Balsamic Vinaigrette Dressing
Duck Salad with Orange Zest served with a
Basket of Pita Chips
Michigan Cherry Cheese Tart—Chocolate Mousse Torte
Orange Curd Tartlets—Chocolate Chip Cookies
Sugared Grapes—Walnut Diamonds

Sunday, August 20, 2000
3:00 to 6:00 p.m.

Catering
Opus One

Musical Performance
John MacElwee Jazz Trio

Appetizers

Mushroom Nut Pâté

1   onion, chopped
1   garlic clove, crushed
1   tablespoon sunflower oil
1   cup chopped white mushrooms
3/4   cup chopped cashews or walnuts
5   ounces cream cheese, softened
2   tablespoons water
1   tablespoon dry sherry
1   tablespoon soy sauce
    Dash of Worcestershire sauce
    Salt and pepper to taste
    Chopped fresh parsley
    Dash of paprika

Sauté the onion and garlic in the sunflower oil in a skillet until the onion is translucent. Cool slightly. Process the onion mixture, mushrooms, cashews, cream cheese, water, sherry, soy sauce, Worcestershire sauce, salt and pepper in a food processor until coarsely puréed. Adjust the seasonings to taste.

Spoon into a serving bowl. Chill, covered, in the refrigerator. Garnish with fresh parsley and a dash of paprika just before serving. Serve with your favorite crackers.

Serves 6 to 8

Minka's Phyllo Mushroom Appetizers

2 1/2   pounds mushrooms, chopped
    Butter
    Salt to taste
2   bunches green onions
    Vegetable oil
12   ounces cream cheese, softened
    Pepper to taste
1   cup (2 sticks) butter
1   (16-ounce) package phyllo

Simmer the mushrooms in a small amount of butter and salt to taste in a skillet until the liquid has almost evaporated. Sauté the green onions in a small amount of oil in a small skillet until tender. Add the sautéed green onions and cream cheese to the mushrooms. Cook over low heat until the cream cheese melts and the mixture is neither too thick nor too thin, stirring constantly. Season with salt and pepper to taste.

Melt 1 cup butter in a saucepan over low heat. Unroll the phyllo and place the entire stack on a clean flat surface, keeping covered with a damp cloth to prevent drying out. Remove the top phyllo sheet and place on a clean flat surface; brush with the melted butter. Stack another phyllo sheet on top of the first one; brush with melted butter. Top with another phyllo sheet. Sprinkle the top evenly with the mushroom mixture. Roll up the stack and arrange in a 10×14-inch baking pan. Repeat the process with the remaining phyllo and mushroom mixture until all of the ingredients are used. Bake at 350 degrees for 45 to 60 minutes or until golden brown. Cut each roll-up into 2- to 3-inch pieces.

Serves about 20

Doug's Vegetarian Grape Leaves

3	cups Italian rice		Salt, pepper and coriander to taste
7	cups chopped onions		
1/2	cup olive oil	1 1/2	to 2 pounds fresh grape leaves
1	bunch fresh parsley, finely chopped		Boiling water
1	bunch fresh dill, finely chopped	2	cups water
	Juice of 1 lemon		Olive oil
			Lemon slices

Soak the rice in enough water to cover in a saucepan for 1 hour; drain. Squeeze the chopped onions with your hands to soften. Combine the rice, onions, olive oil, parsley, dill, lemon juice, salt, pepper and coriander in a bowl and mix well. Soak the grape leaves in boiling water in a saucepan for a few minutes; drain. Cut off the stems. Spread some of the leaves in the bottom of an 8-quart saucepan.

Arrange 1 of the remaining leaves back side up with the stem end facing you on a small plate. Place a teaspoonful of the rice filling near the stem end. Fold the leaf over the sides to enclose the filling and roll up beginning at the stem end. Repeat the process with the remaining grape leaves and filling.

Arrange the roll-ups side by side in the prepared pan in 2, 3 or 4 layers. Place a plate over the top to keep the roll-ups in place. Add 2 cups water. Cook, covered, over low heat for 1 1/2 hours. Let stand, covered with the plate, until cool to prevent discoloration. Sprinkle the roll-ups with olive oil for a shiny appearance and/or garnish with lemon slices. Serve at room temperature.

Makes 70 to 100 appetizers

Note: If you are using canned grape leaves, rinse in boiling water before using. You may also place the roll-ups in a prepared 8-quart baking dish, add the water, cover with a plate and bake at 350 degrees for 1 1/2 hours.

Robert Pangborn, DSO principal percussionist, who, when he was a member of the Cleveland Orchestra, heard this account from Etienne Gluck during the late 1950s.

The late George Szell, music director of the Cleveland Orchestra from 1946 to 1970, enjoyed cooking, as well as golf, as a favorite off-the-podium pastime. He owned a kitchen apron, which must have seemed laughably incongruous when worn by this notoriously dictatorial conductor. It said "Whoo-pee" across the front. Not far from his residence in the upscale Cleveland suburb of Shaker Heights was an excellent French restaurant called Chef Etienne's, which Szell would occasionally patronize. When dining there, he often indulged his culinary interests by going into the kitchen to observe. Etienne Gluck, the owner and chef, generally tolerated these intrusions by the world-famous musician. However, Szell overstepped Etienne's good graces one evening when he dipped a spoon into the pan, tasted a sauce, and began offering suggestions on how to make it even better. Szell was politely escorted out of the kitchen by the chef, who offered his own advice, "Maestro, you take care of zee Beethoven, and I will take care of the zee Béarnaise!"

Appetizers

Portobello Pizza with Andouille and Roasted Peppers

Portobello Mushrooms

4   (4-ounce) portobello mushrooms
1/4 cup olive oil
1/4 teaspoon salt
1/8 teaspoon pepper

Andouille and Roasted Pepper Filling

8   ounces andouille sausage
1/2 cup chopped red bell pepper, sautéed
1   cup shredded mozzarella cheese
1   egg
1   tablespoon chopped fresh chives
     Pinch of salt
1/2 cup bread crumbs

For the mushrooms, remove the stems from the mushrooms and reserve for another use. Scrape the underside of the mushrooms clean using a tablespoon. Brush the top and bottom of the mushroom caps with olive oil. Season with salt and pepper. Arrange on a grill rack. Grill until tender but still firm. Remove to a baking sheet.

For the filling, process the sausage in a food processor until coarsely chopped. Add the sautéed bell pepper, cheese, egg, chives, salt and bread crumbs and process until incorporated.

To assemble, fill the grilled mushroom caps with the stuffing mixture. Bake at 400 degrees for 8 to 10 minutes or until hot and golden brown.

Serves 4

Variations

For Portobello Pizza with Pesto and Roma Tomatoes, prepare and grill the mushrooms as described at left. To make the pesto, process 2 garlic cloves, 1 cup packed fresh basil leaves and 1/4 cup lightly toasted pine nuts in a food processor until smooth. Add 1/4 cup olive oil, 1/4 cup grated Parmesan cheese and 1/4 teaspoon salt, processing constantly. Spread the pesto in the mushroom caps. Top each with 3 to 4 slices Roma tomatoes. Sprinkle with 1/4 cup grated Parmesan cheese. Bake as directed.

For Portobello Pizza with Spinach and Feta Cheese, prepare and grill the mushrooms as described at left. To make the spinach and feta filling, sauté 1 teaspoon minced shallots and 1 teaspoon minced garlic in 1 teaspoon clarified butter in a large skillet over high heat. Add 1 pound spinach, rinsed. Cook until the spinach is wilted. Remove from the heat. Season with salt and pepper to taste. Let stand until cool. Squeeze out any excess moisture. Fill the mushroom caps with the spinach mixture. Sprinkle with crumbled feta cheese. Bake as directed.

Funghi Ripieni
(Stuffed Mushrooms)

12   *large mushrooms*
1   *tablespoon olive oil*
1   *garlic clove, finely chopped*
1/2 *cup finely chopped yellow onion*
2   *tablespoons chopped fresh parsley*
1/2 *cup fresh bread crumbs*
1   *cup chopped cooked bacon or ham (optional)*
1/2 *cup grated Parmesan cheese*
     Salt and pepper to taste
     Chicken broth
     Olive oil
     Chopped fresh parsley, grated Parmesan cheese

Clean the mushrooms and remove the stems, reserving the caps. Chop the mushroom stems. Heat 1 tablespoon olive oil in a skillet. Add the mushroom stems, garlic and onion. Sauté for 5 minutes. Stir in the parsley, bread crumbs, bacon, 1/2 cup Parmesan cheese, salt and pepper. Add just enough chicken broth to bind the mixture together. Spoon into the mushroom caps. Pour a small amount of olive oil in a shallow baking dish. Arrange the stuffed mushrooms in a single layer in the prepared dish. Sprinkle with a small amount of olive oil. Bake at 375 degrees for 20 minutes. Garnish with chopped fresh parsley and grated Parmesan cheese. Serve hot.

Makes 12

Black Tie and Orchids
Bloomfield Hills

Travel in time through a house of contrasts—dance for hours in an elegant Gatsbyesque ballroom, descend the medieval staircase and dine in an authentic colonial tavern.

Saturday, June 1, 1991
7:00 p.m.

Hosts
Mr. and Mrs. Robert Allesee
Mr. and Mrs. James Holmes

Menu
Hors d'oeuvres
Stuffed Mushrooms (at left)
Shrimp Puffs
Bacon Marinated in Chutney
Spinach Quiche
Entrée
Beef Tenderloin and Chicken Normandy
Vegetable Medley
Wild Rice
Dessert
Exquisite Sweets

Open Bar and Appropriate Wines

Music
Mack Pitt Orchestra (Three hours dance music)

Flowers
The Orchid Garden of Joyce Hague
(An orchid corsage for each lady)

Appetizers

Cocktail Meatballs

Meatballs

2   pounds ground round
1   cup bread crumbs
1   envelope onion soup mix
3   eggs, beaten

Sauce

1   (12-ounce) bottle chili sauce
3/4 cup water
1   cup packed light brown sugar
1   pound sauerkraut, drained (2 cups)
1   cup whole cranberry sauce

For the meatballs, combine the ground round, bread crumbs, onion soup mix and eggs in a large bowl and mix well. Shape into 70 meatballs.

For the sauce, combine the chili sauce, water, brown sugar, sauerkraut and cranberry sauce in a bowl and mix well.

To assemble, arrange the meatballs in a 9×13-inch baking pan. Spread the sauce over the meatballs. Bake at 350 degrees for 2 hours.

Makes 70 meatballs

Note: This recipe may be assembled ahead and frozen. Thaw before baking.

Marinated Grilled Peppers with Olives and Anchovies

3   medium red bell peppers
2   to 4 oil-pack anchovies, drained, cut into 1/4-inch pieces
2   tablespoons drained rinsed capers
4   fresh basil leaves, thinly slivered
1/4 cup niçoise or other oil-cured black olives
1   tablespoon balsamic vinegar, or to taste
1/4 cup extra-virgin olive oil
     Kosher or sea salt and freshly ground pepper to taste

Arrange the bell peppers on a grill rack. Grill over high heat until evenly blackened over the entire surface, turning frequently. Remove to a paper bag and close. Let stand until cool. Remove the skin from the bell peppers and discard the seeds and core. Chop the bell peppers into 1/2-inch pieces.

Combine the bell peppers, anchovies, capers, basil, olives, balsamic vinegar, olive oil, kosher salt and pepper in a bowl and mix well. Marinate at room temperature for 15 minutes before serving.

Serves 4 to 6

Mulled Cider

4	cups water	2	tablespoons candied ginger
2	cups sugar	4	cups orange juice
6	whole cloves	1	cup lemon juice
4	cinnamon sticks	1/2	gallon cider
4	whole allspice		

Combine the water, sugar, cloves, cinnamon sticks, allspice and ginger in a saucepan. Bring to a boil. Boil for 10 minutes. Remove from the heat. Cover and let stand for 1 hour to blend flavors. Strain the mixture into a large saucepan, discarding the whole spices. Add the orange juice, lemon juice and cider. Heat until ready to serve.

Serves 36

Note: You may purchase cider in the fall and keep frozen until ready to use.

Saint Patrick's Day Whiskey

1 1/2	jiggers Tulamore Dew or Black Bush Irish Whiskey	2	(6- or 8-ounce) wine glasses
		2	ice cubes

Pour the whiskey into 1 of the wine glasses. Add the ice cubes. Stir gently, twice up and down, 10 times to the left and 10 times to the right. Remove the ice cubes. Fill the remaining wine glass with water. Sip the whiskey and follow with the water.

Serves 1

Johannes Brahms
German Composer
(1833–1897)

A great wine connoisseur invited Brahms to dinner and in his honor brought out some of his choicest bottles. "This is the Brahms of my cellar," he announced to the company as wine from a venerable bottle was poured into the composer's glass. Brahms scrutinized the wine closely, inhaled its bouquet, took a sip, and then put down his glass without comment. "How do you like it?" anxiously asked the host. "Better bring out your Beethoven," murmured Brahms.

Overtures

Soups & Salads

Soups

Sonata at Sunset

Enjoy a succulent dinner at a summer mecca on the sands of Lake Michigan. View the setting sun descending into the lake waters, creating a tapestry of color to the accompaniment of the lapping waves blending their beach music with our DSO musicians as you sip after dinner drinks. Dancing in the moonlight is an option you won't want to miss!

Tuesday, July 6, 1999
6:00 p.m.

Your Hosts
Gloria and Stan Nycek
Millie and Lowell Everson

Menu
Hors d'oeuvres
Cocktails
Fresh Peach Soup Alexander (at right)
Ballottine of Pork
Farci of Apricots, Cranberries, Porcini Mushrooms
and Herbs, served with a Buttered Cider Sauce
Tiny New Potatoes
Green Beans sautéed in Garlic
Tender Fresh Greens Garnished with Michigan Dried
Cherries, Walnuts and Perla's Secret Dressing
Homemade Crescent Rolls
Trio of Chocolate Mousse on a Raspberry Coulis

Coffee and Tea
After Dinner Drinks

Wines will be selected to complement the menu

Musical Performance
The De Villen Quartet
Philip Dikeman, Flute
Laura Rowe, Violin
Caroline Coade, Viola
Alicia Rowe, Cello

Fresh Peach Soup Alexander

6   ripe peaches, peeled, pitted
1/4   cup packed brown sugar
1/4   cup cream sherry
1 1/2 cups reduced-fat vanilla yogurt
      Sprigs of fresh mint or fresh blueberries

Purée the peaches in a food processor. Add the brown sugar and sherry and blend well. Pour into a bowl. Chill, covered, for 8 to 12 hours. Stir in the yogurt just before serving. Ladle into serving bowls. Garnish with fresh mint or blueberries.

Serves 6

S o u p s

Cold Emerald Soup with Rosemary Croutons

Emerald Soup

4   cups chicken stock
1/2   envelope cream of leek soup mix
1   (10-ounce) package frozen chopped broccoli
4   or 5 sprigs of fresh parsley
      Dash of Worcestershire sauce
1/2   cup heavy cream

Rosemary Croutons

2   tablespoons butter
1/8   teaspoon salt
1/4   teaspoon rosemary
2   cups corn, rice or wheat Chex

For the soup, combine the chicken stock, soup mix and broccoli in a 2-quart saucepan. Bring to a boil and reduce the heat. Add the parsley and Worcestershire sauce. Simmer until the broccoli is tender. Process in a blender until puréed. Pour into a large bowl. Add the cream and mix well. Chill, covered, in the refrigerator.

For the croutons, melt the butter in a shallow sauté pan. Add the salt and rosemary and mix well. Add the cereal and toss to coat. Continue to cook until the cereal is heated through, stirring constantly. Remove from the heat and cool. Store in an airtight container.

To serve, ladle the cold soup into serving bowls. Sprinkle with the croutons.

Serves 6

Roasted Tomato Bisque

2   ounces chopped garlic
1   large onion, chopped
6   ribs celery, chopped
1   bunch leeks, chopped
1   cup (2 sticks) unsalted butter
12   tomatoes, roasted
8   ounces tomato paste
8   ounces tomato purée
4   to 6 cups chicken stock
2   bay leaves
6   black peppercorns
      Salt and pepper to taste
2   cups cream

Sauté the garlic, onion, celery and leeks in the butter in a large skillet until the onion is translucent. Add the roasted tomatoes, tomato paste and tomato purée and mix well. Add enough chicken stock to make the desired consistency, stirring constantly. Add the bay leaves, peppercorns, salt and pepper and mix well. Simmer for 45 minutes. Blend in batches in a food processor. Pour the soup through a strainer into a large bowl, discarding the solids. Stir in the cream. Ladle into serving bowls.

Serves 8 to 10

Soups

Crab Bisque

1   (10-ounce) can cream of mushroom soup
1   (10-ounce) can cream of asparagus soup
2   cups milk
1   cup half-and-half
1   (6-ounce) can crab meat, drained, flaked
1/3   cup dry white wine or sherry
1   teaspoon salt
1   teaspoon pepper

Combine the mushroom soup, asparagus soup, milk and half-and-half in a saucepan and mix well. Cook until heated through, stirring constantly. Add the crab meat and wine and mix well. Season with the salt and pepper. Ladle into soup bowls.

Serves 6 to 8

New England Clam Chowder

1/3   pound sliced bacon, cut into halves
2   medium or large onions, thinly sliced
1 1/2 cups water
2   medium or large potatoes, cut into 1-inch pieces
4   cups milk
2   (7-ounce) cans minced clams, drained
1/2   cup (1 stick) butter

Cook the bacon in a skillet until crisp; drain thoroughly. Boil the onions in the water in a large saucepan until tender. Add the potatoes. Boil to form a thick purée with practically no water remaining, stirring frequently. Add the milk. Bring to a low boil. Add the bacon, clams and butter. Cook until the butter melts, stirring constantly. Ladle into soup bowls.

Serves 4 to 6

White Corn Chowder

1/4   cup (1/2 stick) butter
1   medium onion
3   ribs celery, chopped
2   carrots, chopped
2   tablespoons flour
2   cups chicken broth
4   cups milk
2   medium potatoes, chopped, cooked
3   cups whole kernel white corn
     Salt and pepper to taste

Melt the butter in a heavy stockpot. Add the onion, celery and carrots. Cook over medium heat until tender. Sprinkle with the flour. Cook for 3 minutes, stirring frequently. Stir in the chicken broth and milk. Cook until steaming. Add the cooked potatoes and corn. Cook over low heat for 45 to 55 minutes, stirring occasionally. Season with salt and pepper. Ladle into soup bowls.

Serves 4 to 6

Meatless Chili

3	large onions, finely chopped (about 3 cups)
6	large garlic cloves, minced (about 2 tablespoons)
1/4	cup olive oil
3	(28-ounce) cans diced tomatoes in purée
5	tablespoons dark brown sugar
2	tablespoons unsulphured dark molasses
2	tablespoons chili powder
1	tablespoon cumin
3	tablespoons oregano
1	teaspoon coriander
1/8	teaspoon ground allspice
3	cups chopped green bell peppers (about 3)
3	cups chopped carrots
3	cups chopped celery
1	small jalapeño, minced
5	(4-ounce) cans chopped green chiles
3	(15-ounce) cans pinto beans, rinsed, drained (about 5 to 6 cups)
	Salt to taste

Sauté the onions and garlic in the olive oil in a large stockpot until tender but not brown. Add the tomatoes, brown sugar, molasses, chili powder, cumin, oregano, coriander and allspice and mix well. Bring to a boil and reduce the heat. Simmer, covered, for 45 to 60 minutes. Add the bell peppers, carrots, celery, jalapeño and green chiles. Simmer for 40 minutes. Add the beans and salt. Simmer for 5 minutes longer. Remove from the heat and cool. Chill in the refrigerator for 1 day. Divide into smaller freezer containers and freeze for at least 3 to 7 days or for up to 1 month or longer to enhance the flavor. Reheat to serve and adjust the seasonings.

Serves 20 to 25

Note: This recipe must be frozen for at least 3 days before serving in order to enhance the flavor. If you prefer beef in your chili, brown 3 pounds of lean chopped beef before adding the onions.

Pablo Picasso had his blue period, Igor Stravinsky had his neoclassical period, and DSO Clarinetist Doug Cornelson, had his hot dog period, a time when his preferred lunch choice was the famous American coney or hot dog. (Doug is now almost a vegetarian. Time and diets change.) On the European tour of 1979 with Antal Dorati, Doug found himself in Madrid, Spain, ordering lunch in a neighborhood cafe. Linguistically he was unable to communicate with anyone, futilely struggling with English, then his nearly nonexistent Spanish, and then sign language for a few embarrassing minutes. He finally was successful in making his lunch order understood when he took a paper napkin from a dispenser and, with a ballpoint pen from his jacket pocket, drew a picture of a hot dog. The waiter's expression changed from frustration to smiling comprehension, and in a few minutes Doug had his hot dog. The beverage was easy. Coffee is "cafe" almost everywhere in Europe.

Soups

White Hat Chicken Chili

4   boneless skinless chicken breasts
2¹/2 cups reduced-fat chicken broth
1   teaspoon lemon pepper
1   garlic clove, finely chopped
1   cup chopped onion
2   (8-ounce) cans white Shoe Peg corn, drained
2   (4-ounce) cans chopped green chiles, drained
1   teaspoon cumin
¹/8   teaspoon ground cloves
¹/8   teaspoon cayenne pepper
2   to 3 tablespoons lime juice
2   (14-ounce) cans white or Great Northern beans
1¹/2 cups tortilla chips
1   cup shredded reduced-fat Monterey Jack cheese
     Salsa
¹/4   cup chopped fresh cilantro
     Sour cream

Cut the chicken into bite-size pieces. Cook the chicken in a large skillet sprayed with nonstick cooking spray until brown and cooked through. Combine the chicken broth and lemon pepper in a large saucepan. Bring to a boil. Add the chicken.

Spray the skillet again with nonstick cooking spray. Add the garlic. Sauté over low heat for 1 minute. Do not brown the garlic. Add to the chicken mixture. Add the onion to the skillet. Sauté until tender. Add the onion, corn, green chiles, cumin, cloves, cayenne pepper and lime juice to the chicken mixture. Bring to a boil. Add the beans and reduce the heat. Simmer for 45 minutes or until heated through.

To serve, ladle the hot chili over the tortilla chips and cheese in serving bowls. Serve with salsa, cilantro and sour cream.

Serves 8 to 10

Beef Soup

1¹/2 pounds stew beef
1   teaspoon salt
¹/2   teaspoon pepper
2   bay leaves
4   or 5 medium carrots, sliced
¹/2   cup chopped onion
1   cup chopped celery
1   cup chopped cabbage
2¹/2 cups canned Italian tomatoes
1   tablespoon Worcestershire sauce
1   beef bouillon cube
     Pinch of oregano
¹/4   cup barley

Place the beef in a heavy 3-quart stockpot and cover with water. Add the salt, pepper and bay leaves. Bring to a boil. Add the carrots, onion, celery and cabbage. Reduce the heat to low. Simmer, covered, for 2¹/2 hours or until the beef is very tender. Remove the bay leaves. Add the tomatoes, Worcestershire sauce, bouillon cube, oregano and barley. Simmer, covered, for 1¹/2 hours. Ladle into soup bowls.

Serves 6

Gershwin's Greatest Gumbo

A New Orleans favorite.

4   Cornish game hens, cooked
3/4 cup vegetable oil
1   cup bleached flour
2   cups chopped yellow onions
1   cup chopped green bell pepper
1/2 cup chopped celery
1   teaspoon salt
1   teaspoon cayenne pepper
3   bay leaves
2   teaspoons minced garlic (optional)
8   cups chicken stock
1   pound cooked smoked sausage, sliced
1/2 cup chopped green onions
2   tablespoons chopped fresh parsley
     Hot cooked rice

Chop the hens, discarding the skin and bones. Set aside. Combine the oil and flour in a large saucepan. Cook over medium heat for 30 minutes or until the roux is dark brown, stirring constantly. Add the onions, bell pepper, celery, salt, cayenne pepper and bay leaves. Cook over medium heat for 10 minutes or until the vegetables are tender, stirring frequently. Add the chopped hens and garlic. Cook for 5 minutes. Add the chicken stock and sausage. Bring to a boil and reduce the heat to medium. Cook for 5 minutes. Reduce the heat to a simmer. Simmer for 1 hour. Skim off any grease from the top. Discard the bay leaves. Stir in the green onions and parsley. Ladle over hot cooked rice into serving bowls.

Serves 8 to 10

A Gershwin Gala
Rochester Hills

Celebrate the 100th year of the birth of George Gershwin, the younger brother of the dynamic composer/lyricist duo, considered to be among the most colorful creators of the greatest theater music in the world.

Enjoy the melding of Gershwin classics with the ambiance of a music room that replicates a theatrical sound stage! Showcased in a nearly 2,000-square-foot, two-story music room with period original and reproduction furnishings, three reproducing grand pianos, and a reproducing three-manual pipe organ will delight your senses.

This tribute to Gershwin reflects the infectious vitality, flair-for-living and elegance of an exquisite personality from a bygone era. Mark your calendar, so that you can savor the moment in what promises to be a most captivating evening!

Saturday, August 15th, 1998
7:30 p.m. - 10:30 p.m.

Your Hosts
John Fischer and James Weisenborne

Menu
Passed Hors d'oeuvres
Spicy Grilled Shrimp
Fresh Asparagus Tartlets with Chives
Mushroom Pâté Bites—Roquefort and Mascarpone Puffs
Quesadilla Wedges with Grilled Chicken Breast, Mango Salsa and Grilled Onions
Smoked Salmon on Toast Rounds with Dill Mustard Sauce, Minced Onions and Capers
Marinated Eggplant and Roasted Peppers on Toasted Fresh Bread with Fresh Basil
Beef Tenderloin Wrapped Asparagus Tips with Horseradish Herb Cheese
Set-Out Desserts
Mini Raspberry Tarts—Lemon Meringue Tarts
Chocolate Truffle Triangles—Pecan Diamonds
Chocolate-Dipped Strawberries
Chocolate Fantasy with Champagne
Choo-Choo's Chocolates of Oxford
served at 10:00 p.m.
Beverages
White Wine—Champagne—Sparkling Water

Soup and a Sonorous Soirée

With the Detroit Symphony Orchestra Hall Staff
Grosse Pointe

Enjoy a late and leisurely afternoon of full-bodied soups, scintillating conversation and the thrills and trills of the woodwinds!

You are cordially invited to join the executive staffpersons of the DSO and their special guest-of-honor, DSO Music Director Neeme Järvi, at a lovely Grosse Pointe home.

While sipping soups and spirits, here is a golden opportunity to ask your hosts all that your heart desires about the orchestra and its long, rich history. By the way, how did former DSO Director Ossip Gabrilowitsch actually meet his wife—the daughter of Mark Twain?

Sunday, September 28, 1997
3:00 p.m.

Your Hosts

Virginia Fallis, Herbert Ferrer, Christie Peck, Dawn Saxton, Sally Slater and Jill Woodward

Menu

Appetizers
Selection of Mini Quiches, Chicken Liver Pâté
Assorted Cheeses, Crudité

Main (Soup) Course
Potato Garlic Soup—Ginger and Lentil Soup
Seafood Gumbo—Cold Carrot Soup
Mixed Green Salad with Assorted Dressings
Variety of Breads and Bread Sticks

Desserts
Cold Watermelon Soup
Double-Decadent Chocolate Brownie Torte
Fruit Salad, Lemon Bars, Pecan Pie

Beverages
Selection of Wines, Soda and Sparkling Water
Coffee and Tea

Music by DSO Woodwind Quintet, featuring Ervin Monroe, flute; Donald Baker, oboe; Theodore Oien, clarinet; Robert Williams, bassoon; and Eugene Wade, French horn

Tom's Minestrone

2	tablespoons olive oil
3	garlic cloves, minced
2	ribs celery with leaves, chopped
2	carrots, chopped
1	large onion, chopped
1	green bell pepper, chopped
4	cups mushrooms, sliced
2	tomatoes, chopped
1	teaspoon each rosemary, marjoram and thyme
6	cups beef, chicken or vegetable stock
1/4	cup dry sherry
1/4	cup red wine
1	tablespoon Worcestershire sauce
1/4	teaspoon Tabasco sauce
1	cup tiny new red potatoes
1	large zucchini, chopped
1/2	cup uncooked macaroni
	Salt and pepper to taste
1/2	cup minced fresh parsley
	Freshly grated Parmesan cheese

Heat the olive oil in a Dutch oven or large stockpot over medium heat. Add the garlic, celery, carrots, onion and bell pepper. Cook for 5 minutes or until softened. Add the mushrooms and tomatoes. Cook for 10 minutes or until the vegetables are fragrant. Add the rosemary, marjoram, thyme, stock, sherry, red wine, Worcestershire sauce and Tabasco sauce. Bring to a boil and reduce the heat. Simmer for 1 hour or until the vegetables are tender. Add the potatoes, zucchini and uncooked macaroni. Cook for 10 minutes or until tender. Season with salt and pepper to taste. Serve with a generous sprinkle of parsley and pass the Parmesan cheese at the table.

Serves 4 to 6

Soups

Broccoli Soup

2   cups heavy cream
3¹/2 cups milk
1¹/2 cups chopped fresh broccoli
¹/4   cup chopped celery
3   tablespoons chopped onion
¹/2   cup (1 stick) butter
1   tablespoon flour
¹/4   teaspoon salt
¹/8   teaspoon white pepper

Bring the cream and milk to a simmer in a heavy saucepan. Add the broccoli, celery and onion. Cook until the vegetables are tender.

Melt the butter in a small saucepan. Stir in the flour to form a roux. Add to the broccoli mixture. Cook for 3 minutes or until thickened, stirring constantly. Remove from the heat. Season with salt and white pepper. Ladle into soup bowls.

Serves 6

Tortellini Soup

2   pounds freshly ground Italian sausage
2   garlic cloves, minced
1   medium onion, chopped
3   large carrots, sliced
4   cups chopped fresh tomatoes
3¹/2 cups tomato sauce
6   cups beef broth
1   cup water
2   tablespoons oregano
2   teaspoons basil
2   tablespoons parsley
1   bay leaf
2   medium zucchini, sliced
2   (10-ounce) packages trio tortellini
      Grated asiago or Parmesan cheese

Brown the sausage in an 8-quart stockpot, stirring until crumbly; drain. Add the garlic, onion, carrots, tomatoes, tomato sauce, beef broth, water, oregano, basil, parsley and bay leaf. Bring to a boil and reduce the heat. Simmer for 2 to 3 hours. Add the zucchini and pasta. Cook for 45 minutes longer. Remove the bay leaf. Ladle into soup bowls. Sprinkle with grated asiago or Parmesan cheese.

Serves 6 to 8

Note: You may substitute one 28-ounce can chopped tomatoes for the fresh. If you prefer a thinner soup, use only 1¹/2 packages tortellini.

S o u p s

Senegalese Soup

Chicken Stock

Chicken bones
1 onion
1/2 bunch celery
1 to 2 carrots
3 peppercorns
2 bay leaves
3 whole cloves

Soup

8 cups Chicken Stock (above)
1 teaspoon curry powder
Chicken fat
Salt and pepper to taste
1/2 cup hot roux
2 cups heavy cream
1/4 cup chopped Granny Smith apple

For the stock, use enough chicken bones to fill your stockpot 3/4 full. Place the bones in a roaster. Add the onion, celery, carrots, peppercorns, bay leaves and cloves. Bake at 350 degrees until the bones are brown, turning the bones every 20 minutes.

Remove the bones to a stockpot, reserving the drippings in the roaster. Remove the fat from the drippings. Add some water to the drippings. Cook over medium-high heat, stirring to deglaze the roaster. Pour into the stockpot. Add enough cold water to cover the bones by 4 inches. Bring to a boil and reduce the heat. Simmer for 2 to 4 hours. Strain the stock into a container, discarding the bones and solid particles. Chill in the refrigerator until a fat cap forms on top. Remove the fat from the top.

For the soup, pour 8 cups of the prepared stock into a stockpot. Bring to a boil and reduce the heat. Heat the curry powder in a small amount of chicken fat in a skillet for 30 seconds. Add to the stock. Simmer for 30 minutes. Season with salt and pepper. Add the hot roux. Simmer for 10 minutes or until thickened, stirring frequently. Strain the soup into a large bowl, discarding the solid particles. Chill, covered, in the refrigerator.

To serve, place the soup in a serving bowl. Add enough cream to make of the desired consistency. Ladle into soup bowls. Add chopped apple to the top of each serving.

Serves 8

Mushroom Barley Soup

1   pound fresh mushrooms
1/4   cup (1/2 stick) butter
1   cup chopped onion
1   garlic clove, minced
3   cups beef broth
6   cups water
3   tablespoons tomato paste
1   teaspoon salt
      Freshly ground pepper to taste
1   bay leaf
1/2   cup barley
1/4   cup chopped fresh parsley
1 1/2 cups chopped celery with leaves
1 1/2 cups chopped carrots
2   tablespoons butter
1/4   cup dry sherry or port
2   cups sour cream

Wipe the mushrooms clean with a damp cloth or brush. Chop 1/2 of the mushrooms. Cut the remaining mushrooms into slices. Melt 1/4 cup butter in a large saucepan. Add the chopped mushrooms, onion and garlic. Sauté until the onion is transparent. Stir in the broth, water, tomato paste, salt, pepper and bay leaf. Bring to a boil. Stir in the barley. Reduce the heat to low. Simmer, covered, for 1 hour.

Add the parsley, celery and carrots. Cook, covered, for 30 minutes or until the carrots and barley are tender. Melt 2 tablespoons butter in a medium skillet. Add the sliced mushrooms. Sauté for 5 minutes. Add the sautéed mushrooms and wine to the barley mixture. Remove the bay leaf. Ladle into soup bowls. Top with a dollop of the sour cream.

Serves 8

Emil Kang
President and Executive Director
Detroit Symphony Orchestra
(2000–)

Emil Kang, with degrees in
business, economics, and violin
performance, brings youth and
talent to a very challenging position.
He is still practicing his culinary
skills, however. Miyeuk soup, made
from fresh seaweed, is very common
in Korea and is traditionally served
in honor of a person's birthday.
Emil says, "When my sister and
I were in our pre-teen years, we
tried to make this soup for our
father's birthday in an attempt to
provide him with a present we
could afford. Needless to say, our
family ordered pizza that night,
hold the seaweed!"

Mi-Yeuk-Kook (Seaweed Soup)

2	*ounces dried miyeuk (seaweed)*
4	*ounces beef, shredded*
1	*tablespoon sesame oil*
3	*tablespoons soy sauce*
1	*teaspoon minced garlic*
15	*cups water*
1	*teaspoon salt*
	Pepper to taste

Place the seaweed in a bowl and cover with water. Soak for 30 to
50 minutes; drain. Rinse the seaweed until clean. Cut the seaweed
into the desired size. Sauté the beef in the sesame oil in a stockpot for
10 seconds. Add the seaweed, soy sauce and garlic. Simmer for
2 minutes. Add 15 cups water. Bring to a boil over high heat. Boil for
5 minutes. Reduce the heat. Simmer until the seaweed is tender.
Sprinkle with the salt and pepper. Ladle into soup bowls.

Serves 5

Soups

Soupe au Pistou

Soupe

16 cups (3 quarts) chicken stock or water
1   cup chopped smoked bacon
2   leeks (white part only), sliced
1   cup sliced carrots
3/4 cup chopped onion
1   tablespoon olive oil
4   tomatoes, peeled
    Bouquet garni of thyme, rosemary, bay leaf,
        basil and parsley
6   garlic cloves
1   cup kidney beans
1   cup flat peas or flat Italian beans
1   cup haricots blanc or white beans
    Salt and pepper to taste
1   cup string bean pieces
1   cup chopped potato
1   cup chopped baby marrows (squash)
1/3 cup uncooked broken spaghetti

Pistou

2   garlic cloves
1   cup fresh basil leaves
    Olive oil

Assembly

1   cup shredded Gruyère cheese

For the soupe, place the chicken stock and bacon in a 4- or 5-quart stockpot. Cook the leeks, carrots and onion in the olive oil in a skillet until the onions are transparent. Add the tomatoes, bouquet garni and garlic. Add to the chicken stock. Stir in the kidney beans, flat peas and haricots blanc. Bring to a boil. Season with salt and pepper. Add the string beans, potato and baby marrows. Cook until the vegetables are partially cooked through. Add the uncooked pasta. Cook until the pasta is tender.

For the pistou, pound the garlic and basil in a mortar with a pestle. Add a small amount of olive oil, pounding constantly. Pound in 3 tablespoons of the soup to make a soft paste.

To assemble, remove the bouquet garni from the soup. Pour the soup into a tureen. Add the pistou and Gruyère cheese.

Serves 8

Salads

Salads

Eurasian "Spring Roll" Salad

Spring Rolls

4   large round Thai spring roll wrappers
12 fresh cilantro leaves
8   fresh mint leaves
1/2 teaspoon chopped sweet ginger
2   ounces carrot, shredded
2   ounces melon or papaya, julienned
4   ounces soaked bean thread noodles
2   ounces leeks, julienned
2   ounces red bell pepper, julienned

Dressing

4   garlic cloves
2   tablespoons chopped sweet ginger
2   teaspoons chopped fresh cilantro
2   tablespoons lime zest
1/2 cup lime juice
2   tablespoons orange zest
1   cup orange juice
2   tablespoons rice vinegar
1   teaspoon honey
    Chopped chile to taste

Salad and Assembly

4   ounces baby greens
12 pieces Belgian endive
1   ounce enoki mushrooms
12 snow pea pods, steamed, cut into quarters

For the spring rolls, soak the spring roll wrappers in warm water in a bowl. Place 1 wrapper at a time on a towel. Sprinkle each with cilantro, mint and ginger. Layer the carrot, melon, bean thread noodles, leeks and bell pepper over the top. Roll each wrapper up tightly to enclose the filling and cover with plastic wrap.

For the dressing, combine the garlic, ginger, cilantro, lime zest, lime juice, orange zest, orange juice, rice vinegar, honey and chile in a bowl and mix well.

For the salad, place the greens on 4 salad plates. Arrange the endive, enoki mushrooms and snow pea pods over the greens. Drizzle with the dressing. Place a spring roll on each plate.

Serves 4

Note: Chopped sweet ginger is also called pickled ginger.

Fresh Asparagus Salad with Lemon Dijon Vinaigrette

Lemon Dijon Vinaigrette

1	medium lemon
1/4	cup olive oil
2	tablespoons corn oil or canola oil
1/8	teaspoon salt
1/4	teaspoon pepper
1 1/2	teaspoons Dijon mustard

Asparagus Salad

8	ounces asparagus, trimmed
1	slice bacon, cooked, drained, crumbled
4	dry-cured black olives, pitted
	Freshly ground pepper to taste

For the vinaigrette, remove the peel from the lemon. Cut into thin strips. Place in a saucepan and cover with water. Boil for 1 to 2 minutes; drain. Squeeze 3 tablespoons lemon juice into a jar with a tight-fitting lid. Add the lemon peel, olive oil, corn oil, salt, pepper and Dijon mustard. Cover the jar and shake well to mix. Chill until ready to serve.

For the salad, cook the asparagus in enough water to cover in a saucepan for 4 to 5 minutes or until tender but still bright green. Remove with tongs and plunge immediately into ice water to stop the cooking process; drain. Arrange the asparagus on 2 salad plates. Spoon the vinaigrette over the asparagus. Sprinkle with the bacon and olives. Season with freshly ground pepper.

Serves 2

Paradise Theatre

Music was brought back to Orchestra Hall on Christmas Eve, 1941, by new owners, Ben and Lou Cohen. Known as the Paradise Theatre, it would present the best and biggest names in jazz, bebop, and blues for the next ten years. Duke Ellington, Louis Armstrong, Ella Fitzgerald, Billie Holliday, Lena Horne, and other stars performed there. It was named after the area just east of Woodward Avenue called Paradise Valley, an area that was home to a large percentage of Detroit's African-Americans and the main black entertainment district.

In 1950, just before the reorganization of the Detroit Symphony Orchestra under the "Detroit Plan," a very young, and relatively unknown, Leonard Bernstein came to Detroit as a guest conductor and pianist. After the concert, he asked violinist Felix Resnick if it would be possible to hear some of Detroit's famous jazz musicians. With Lare Wardrop, oboist, and Bernard Rosen, clarinetist, Felix took Bernstein to Paradise Valley, where they listened to great jazz until the wee hours of the morning. Musicians and music lovers of all colors were welcomed in the many clubs that lined the streets of the neighborhood in those days. With the end of the big band era, the lure of big money in Las Vegas for entertainers, and the rise of television, the Paradise Theatre closed in 1951.

Salads

Broccoli Salad

1   cup raisins
    Rum or wine
1   bunch broccoli
2   to 3 tablespoons thinly sliced red onion
8   ounces bacon, cooked, drained, crumbled
1/2 cup sunflower seed kernels
1/2 cup mayonnaise
1/4 cup sugar
1/3 cup red wine vinegar or balsamic vinegar
4   to 6 ounces Parmesan cheese, grated

Place the raisins in a bowl. Add enough rum to cover. Let the raisins stand for 1 hour or until plump. Drain the raisins, reserving the liquid.

Trim the stems of the broccoli. Chop the stems and florets into fine pieces. Combine the chopped broccoli, onion, raisins, bacon and sunflower seed kernels in a large bowl and toss to mix. Mix the mayonnaise, sugar, reserved liquid and red wine vinegar in a bowl. Pour over the broccoli mixture and toss to mix well. Sprinkle with the Parmesan cheese.

Serves 6 to 8

Kartoffelsalt
(German Potato Salad)

6   medium to large potatoes
2   tablespoons sugar
2   teaspoons salt
1/8 teaspoon pepper
6   slices bacon, chopped
1   medium onion, chopped
4   cups water
3/4 cup salad oil
3/4 cup apple cider vinegar

Scrub the potatoes and place in a large saucepan. Add enough water to cover. Bring to a boil. Boil until the potatoes are tender; drain. Let stand until cool enough to handle. Peel the potatoes. Cut into slices and place in a large bowl. Add the sugar, salt and pepper.

Cook the bacon in a skillet until crisp. Add the onion. Cook until the onion is translucent; drain. Add to the potatoes. Bring 4 cups water, oil and vinegar to a boil in a saucepan. Pour over the potato mixture and mix well, adding additional hot water if needed for the desired consistency.

Serves 6 to 8

Note: You may chill in the refrigerator and reheat in the oven just before serving.

Indonesian Rice Salad

Dressing

3/4   *cup orange juice*
1/2   *cup safflower oil*
1   *tablespoon sesame oil*
3   *to 4 tablespoons tamari*
2   *tablespoons dry sherry*
      Juice of 1 lemon
1   *to 2 garlic cloves, minced*
1/2   *to 1 teaspoon grated fresh gingerroot*
      Salt and pepper to taste

Rice Salad

2   *cups cooked brown rice, cooled*
1/2   *cup raisins*
2   *cups chopped scallions*
1/4   *cup sesame seeds, toasted*
1/2   *cup thinly sliced water chestnuts*
1   *cup fresh bean sprouts*
1/4   *cup cashews, toasted*
1   *large green bell pepper, chopped*
1   *rib celery, chopped*
      Chopped fresh parsley to taste

For the dressing, combine the orange juice, safflower oil, sesame oil, tamari, sherry, lemon juice, garlic, gingerroot, salt and pepper in a bowl and mix well.

For the salad, combine the rice, raisins, scallions, sesame seeds, water chestnuts, bean sprouts, cashews, bell pepper, celery and parsley in a large bowl. Add the dressing and toss to mix well. Chill, covered, in the refrigerator. Spoon onto lettuce-lined salad plates.

Serves 4 to 6

A James Beard Brunch
Grosse Pointe Farms

The beautiful Grosse Pointe Farms home of interior designer Judith Langenbach provides the backdrop for a fabulous brunch. The home's garden room and garden are featured in this spring's issues of *Better Homes and Gardens/Remodeling* and Detroit's *Style* magazine.

Brunch, prepared by the master chef's friend and colleague, Bill Dollard, will feature a wide range of James Beard's favorite brunch dishes accompanied by outstanding wines and other potables. Bill often assisted Beard in cooking demonstrations around the country and they also cooked together on the several occasions when Jim was Bill's house guest. Join us to enjoy outstanding tastes—in both food and décor.

Menu

Chicken Pâté in Prosciutto Wrap
Parsley Rings
Brillat Savarin and Biscuits
Gazpacho
Pistachio Grapes
Mimosas
Cold Poached Salmon in Aspic with Two Sauces
Vitello Tonnato
Chicken in Lettuce Leaves
Rice Salad (at left)
Bibb Lettuce and Fresh Pea Salad
Rolls and Butter
Fresh Peach Sorbet
Raspberries with Grand Marnier
Crème Anglaise—Madeleines
Coffee and Tea
Wines will be selected to complement the menu

Sunday, July 18, 1999
1:00 p.m.

Your Hosts

Judith and Roy Langenbach
Bill Dollard

Musical Performance

Kimberly Kaloyanides, Violin
Mario DiFiore, Cello

Salads

Korean Salad

Dressing

1/4	cup sugar
1/2	cup vegetable oil
3	tablespoons ketchup
3	tablespoons vinegar
1	tablespoon Worcestershire sauce
1	small onion, grated
	Dash of salt

Salad

1	(16-ounce) package spinach, trimmed
1	(8-ounce) can sliced water chestnuts, drained
2	hard-cooked eggs, cut into small pieces
5	slices bacon, cooked, crumbled
1	(14-ounce) can bean sprouts, drained

For the dressing, process the sugar, oil, ketchup, vinegar, Worcestershire sauce, onion and salt in a blender until smooth.

For the salad, rinse the spinach; drain. Combine the spinach, water chestnuts, hard-cooked eggs, bacon and bean sprouts in a bowl and toss to mix well. Add the dressing and toss to coat.

Serves 8

Salade de Flageolets

Flageolets are small white beans.

2	cups dried flageolets
2	shallots, chopped
1/2	cup chopped fresh parsley
	Olive oil
	Dash of lemon juice
4	lettuce leaves

Sort and rinse the flageolets. Cook the flageolets using the package directions. Let stand until cool. Combine the flageolets, shallots and parsley in a large bowl. Add a small amount of olive oil and the lemon juice and stir to mix well. Line 4 salad plates with the lettuce leaves. Spoon the flageolet mixture over the lettuce leaves.

Serves 4

Note: Use the olive oil and lemon juice sparingly so as not to overwhelm the taste of the flageolets.

Mediterranean Chopped Salad

1	large red bell pepper
1	large Greek pita (pocketless)
1	tablespoon olive oil
	Pinch of salt
1	garlic clove, minced
1/4	cup each chopped fresh parsley, fresh mint and chopped fresh basil
1/3	cup fresh lemon juice
1/2	cup olive oil
1	cup finely chopped romaine
1	large cucumber, peeled, chopped
1	(14-ounce) can garbanzo beans, drained
2	Roma tomatoes, seeded, chopped
1/2	cup chopped purple onion
	Salt and freshly ground pepper to taste
2/3	cup crumbled feta cheese (about 4 ounces)

Place the bell pepper on a baking sheet lined with foil. Broil for 15 minutes or until evenly blackened, turning once or twice. Remove to a bowl and cover with plastic wrap. Let stand until cool. Peel the bell pepper. Remove the seeds and dice the bell pepper.

Brush the pita with 1 tablespoon olive oil. Place on a baking sheet. Broil for 3 minutes on each side or until the edge begins to curl and the pita is firm. Sprinkle with a pinch of salt. Let stand for 5 to 7 minutes to cool. Break the pita into 1/2-inch pieces.

Mix the garlic, parsley, mint, basil and lemon juice in a small bowl. Add 1/2 cup olive oil gradually, whisking constantly.

Combine the romaine, cucumber, roasted bell pepper, garbanzo beans, tomatoes and onion in a large bowl. Add the dressing and toss to coat. Add the pita pieces and toss to mix. Season with salt and pepper to taste. Sprinkle with the feta cheese. Add an extra drizzle of olive oil if desired.

Serves 4

Paul Ganson
DSO Bassoonist and Historian
Restoration
(1970–1989)

When Paul Ganson, DSO bassoonist, heard in 1970 that the long abandoned Orchestra Hall was about to feel the wrecking ball, he decided to do something about it. He rallied other musicians and music lovers to launch the campaign that would eventually restore this acoustically perfect concert hall. The Save Orchestra Hall Association was formed and, for the next nineteen years countless fund-raisers, marches, and rallies were held, and appeals were made to the City of Detroit, the National Trust for Historic Preservation, and the citizens and businesses of Detroit before the project became a reality. Since leaving the Hall in 1939, the Orchestra had played in the Masonic Auditorium, Music Hall, and Ford Auditorium. In 1988, the two organizations got together and formed an alliance that would return the Detroit Symphony to its original home. A year later, on September 15, 1989, a joyous "homecoming" parade of musicians, high school bands, and cheering fans made its way up Woodward Avenue from Ford Auditorium to Orchestra Hall and gave an impromptu concert in the middle of Woodward Avenue.

Cucumber Salad Mold

2	(3-ounce) packages lime gelatin	1	cup mayonnaise
2	cups boiling water	1	teaspoon salt
1/4	cup cider vinegar	1/4	cup grated onion
		2	cups chopped cucumbers

Dissolve the gelatin in the boiling water in a large heatproof bowl. Stir in the vinegar. Chill until set. Whip the gelatin well. Add the mayonnaise, salt, onion and cucumbers and mix well. Spoon into a wet mold to shape. Unmold onto a serving plate.

Serves 6 to 8

Congealed Gazpacho Salad

2	envelopes unflavored gelatin	1/2	cup finely chopped onion
3	cups tomato juice	3/4	cup chopped cucumber, drained
1/4	cup wine vinegar		
1	cup crushed garlic	1/4	cup finely chopped pimentos
2	teaspoons salt		Salad greens
1/4	teaspoon black pepper		Hot peppers
	Dash of cayenne pepper		Dilled okra
2	large tomatoes, chopped, drained	1/2	cup sour cream
		1/2	teaspoon salt
3/4	cup finely chopped green bell pepper	1/3	cup mayonnaise

Soften the gelatin in 1 cup of the tomato juice in a saucepan. Heat until the mixture begins to simmer, stirring constantly. Remove from the heat. Add the remaining tomato juice, vinegar, garlic, 2 teaspoons salt, black pepper and cayenne pepper and mix well. Spoon into a large bowl. Chill until the mixture begins to set. Fold in the tomatoes, bell pepper, onion, cucumber and pimentos. Pour into a 6-cup mold. Chill until set. Unmold onto a plate lined with salad greens. Surround with hot peppers and dilled okra. Mix the sour cream, 1/2 teaspoon salt and mayonnaise in a bowl. Spread over the top.

Serves 8

Salads

Pink Freeze

6   ounces cream cheese, softened
2   tablespoons mayonnaise
2   teaspoons sugar
1   (16-ounce) can whole cranberry sauce
1   (9-ounce) can crushed pineapple, drained
1/2 cup chopped walnuts
1   cup whipping cream, whipped

Beat the cream cheese, mayonnaise and sugar in a mixing bowl until smooth. Add the cranberry sauce, pineapple and walnuts and mix well. Fold in the whipped cream. Spoon into a 4×8-inch loaf pan. Freeze, covered, for 8 to 12 hours. Remove from the freezer and let stand at room temperature for 15 minutes. Cut into slices. Serve on salad plates lined with lettuce leaves.

Serves 12

Blueberry Lime Salad

2   envelopes unflavored gelatin
1   cup cold water
1 1/2 cups hot water
1/2 cup sugar
1/2 cup freshly squeezed lime juice
3   cups fresh blueberries, rinsed, drained

Soften the gelatin in the cold water in a medium bowl. Let stand for 5 minutes. Add the hot water and sugar and stir until the gelatin is dissolved. Stir in the lime juice. Chill until the mixture reaches the consistency of unbeaten egg whites. Fold in the blueberries. Spoon into a 9-inch serving dish. Chill until firm.

Serves 6

Cranberry Salad

2   (3-ounce) packages strawberry gelatin
2   cups boiling water
1   (16-ounce) can whole cranberry sauce
1   cup applesauce
1/2 cup port
1   cup chopped walnuts or other nuts

Dissolve the gelatin in the boiling water in a heatproof bowl. Add the cranberry sauce, applesauce, wine and walnuts and stir to mix well. Pour into a 9×12-inch glass dish. Chill for 8 to 12 hours or until set. Cut into squares and serve on salad plates lined with lettuce.

Serves 12

Salads

Citrus Avocado Salad with Fruit French Dressing

Fruit French Dressing

1/2	cup vegetable oil
2	tablespoons vinegar
2	tablespoons lemon juice
1/2	teaspoon salt
1/4	teaspoon dry mustard
1/4	teaspoon paprika
3	tablespoons confectioners' sugar

Citrus Avocado Salad

2	ripe avocados
2	oranges
2	grapefruit
	Bibb lettuce

For the dressing, combine the oil, vinegar, lemon juice, salt, dry mustard, paprika and confectioners' sugar in a jar with a tight-fitting lid. Cover the jar and shake well. Chill in the refrigerator for 1 hour or longer.

For the salad, peel the avocados and cut into slices. Peel the oranges and grapefruit and separate into sections. Arrange the avocado slices, orange sections and grapefruit sections on a salad plate lined with Bibb lettuce. Shake the dressing and drizzle over the salad.

Serves 6

Coarse Shrimp Coleslaw

1	head napa or savoy cabbage, coarsely chopped
1	small or medium red onion, thinly sliced
1	red bell pepper, cut into thin strips 2 inches long
1	teaspoon mustard seeds
	Salt or seasoned salt to taste
	Pepper to taste
1/2	cup (or more) mayonnaise
1/2	cup (or more) sour cream
	Tabasco sauce to taste
12	ounces (or more) cooked shrimp, peeled, deveined
	Chopped fresh parsley and chopped fresh dill

Combine the cabbage, red onion, bell pepper, mustard seeds, salt and pepper in a bowl and toss to mix.

Mix the mayonnaise, sour cream and Tabasco sauce in a bowl. Add to the cabbage mixture and toss to coat. Add the shrimp and toss to mix. Garnish with chopped fresh parsley and dill.

Serves 4 to 6

Note: You may omit the shrimp or substitute crab meat for the shrimp.

Steak Supper Salad

Mustard Vinaigrette

1	tablespoon Champagne mustard		Sugar to taste
1	teaspoon Pommery mustard		Salt and pepper to taste
1/4	cup white wine vinegar	1/2	cup olive oil

Salad

1/2	cup red wine vinegar	1	pound fresh asparagus
1/4	cup olive oil	1	pound fresh green beans, trimmed
	Freshly ground pepper to taste	1	large red bell pepper, cut into julienne strips
1	(1 1/2- to 2-pound) flank steak		Romaine and leaf lettuce
2	pounds new potatoes		

For the vinaigrette, combine the Champagne mustard, Pommery mustard, white wine vinegar, sugar, salt and pepper in a bowl and mix well. Add the olive oil gradually, whisking constantly.

For the salad, mix the vinegar, olive oil and pepper in a shallow dish. Add the steak. Marinate, covered, in the refrigerator for 3 hours. Drain the steak, discarding the marinade. Place on a grill rack. Grill over high heat until medium-rare. Remove to a platter to cool. Cut the steak into julienne strips. Boil the potatoes in enough water to cover in a saucepan until tender; drain. Let stand until cool enough to handle. Cut into slices. Snap off the tough ends of the asparagus. Add the asparagus to a saucepan filled with boiling water. Cook until tender-crisp. Remove with a spatula and plunge immediately into cold water to stop the cooking process; drain. Repeat the process with the green beans. Cut the blanched asparagus and green beans into 2-inch diagonal pieces.

To assemble, combine the steak, potatoes, asparagus, green beans and bell pepper in a large bowl. Add the vinaigrette and toss to coat. Spoon onto salad plates lined with a bed of romaine and leaf lettuce.

Serves 6

Salads

Chinese Chicken Salad

1 1/2 pounds chopped cooked chicken
1 (16-ounce) package coleslaw with carrots or
      broccoli slaw mix
8 green onions, sliced
3/4 cup seasoned rice vinegar
1/2 cup sugar
1 teaspoon each salt, pepper and MSG
1 cup vegetable oil
1 cup slivered almonds
2 tablespoons vegetable oil
2 (3-ounce) packages ramen noodles
1/4 cup sesame seeds

Combine the chicken, coleslaw and green onions in a large bowl and mix well. Mix the vinegar, sugar, salt, pepper and MSG in a bowl. Add 1 cup oil gradually, whisking constantly. Pour over the chicken mixture and toss to mix well. Chill, covered, for 1 1/2 hours. Sauté the almonds in 2 tablespoons oil in a skillet until brown; drain. Crumble the ramen noodles, reserving the seasoning packets for another use. Add the almonds, ramen noodles and sesame seeds to the chilled chicken mixture and mix well.

Serves 8

Chicken Waldorf Salad

1 large head iceberg lettuce
3 ribs celery, sliced
1 medium bunch red or green seedless grapes
2 ounces walnut pieces
2 Granny Smith apples
12 ounces boneless skinless chicken breasts, cooked,
      cut into julienne strips
   Coleslaw dressing to taste

Rinse the lettuce; drain. Tear the lettuce into bite-size pieces into a large salad bowl. Add the celery, grapes and walnuts. Cut the unpeeled apples into small pieces. Add to the lettuce mixture. Add the chicken strips. Add the desired amount of dressing and toss to coat.

Serves 6

South-of-the-Border Grilled Chicken Salad

*This is a great recipe to take to DSO concerts at Meadow Brook.
Just pack the ingredients in individual containers and
assemble in salad bowls at the concert.*

1/4	cup soy sauce
1/4	cup water
2	tablespoons fresh lime juice
1/2	teaspoon pepper
1/8	teaspoon garlic powder
4	large boneless skinless chicken breasts
1/2	teaspoon pepper
8	cups torn mixed salad greens
3/4	cup mild salsa
1/4	cup buttermilk salad dressing
1	red bell pepper, cut into strips
2	green onions, thinly sliced

Mix the soy sauce, water, lime juice, 1/2 teaspoon pepper and garlic powder in a large shallow container. Add the chicken, turning once. Marinate, covered, in the refrigerator for 6 to 24 hours. Drain the chicken, discarding the marinade. Place on a grill rack. Grill over medium heat for 12 to 15 minutes or until cooked through, turning once. Chill, covered, in the refrigerator. Cut the chicken diagonally into bite-size strips. Season with 1/2 teaspoon pepper.

To assemble, layer the salad greens, salsa, salad dressing, bell pepper, chicken and green onions on a large platter or in individual salad bowls.

Serves 4

Meadow Brook Music Festival

Summertime, and the listening is easy at Meadow Brook Music Festival. Nestled in the hills of the Oakland University campus, this beautiful outdoor setting is the warm weather home of the DSO. Late afternoon finds people putting down their blankets, opening picnic hampers, and preparing for an evening of pure enjoyment. As the sun sets and the stars come out, families and friends relax and listen as the music floats outward from the stage. An occasional bird adding a few blithe notes to the Orchestra's effort is not unusual. Careful programming offers something for everyone, and on family nights, fireworks cap off the festivities.

Main Themes

Meats, Poultry, & Seafood

Meats

M e a t s

Filets Mignons with Tarragon Butter

Tarragon Butter

2 *tablespoons finely minced shallots*
4 *teaspoons butter, softened*
1 *teaspoon tarragon*

Filets Mignons

1 *teaspoon olive oil*
2 *(6-ounce) filets mignons, 2 inches thick*
   Salt and pepper to taste

For the tarragon butter, sauté the shallots in 1 teaspoon of the butter in a skillet for 3 to 4 minutes or just until the shallots begin to brown. Combine with the remaining butter and tarragon in a bowl and mix well. Divide into 2 equal portions. Flatten each portion between sheets of waxed paper. Freeze until firm.

For the filets mignons, heat the olive oil in a cast-iron skillet or ovenproof pan over high heat. Season the filets mignons with salt and pepper. Place in the preheated skillet. Cook until brown on each side. Place the skillet in a 400-degree oven. Bake for 5 minutes for medium-rare. Remove from the oven. Let stand for several minutes before serving. Top with the tarragon butter.

Serves 2

Mrs. Fogarty's West Virginia Barbecue

3   *pounds lean beef and pork*
2   *cups stock*
1/2 *cup chili sauce*
1/2 *cup vinegar*
1/2 *cup sugar*
2   *tablespoons prepared mustard*
1   *garlic clove*
1   *cup minced onion*
2   *tablespoons Worcestershire sauce*

Place the beef and pork in a saucepan. Add the stock and enough water to cover. Bring to a boil and reduce the heat. Simmer until tender; drain. Trim and shred the beef and pork, discarding the skin and bones. Place in a large bowl.

Combine the chili sauce, vinegar, sugar, prepared mustard, garlic, onion and Worcestershire sauce in a saucepan and mix well. Bring to a boil and reduce the heat. Simmer until the onion is tender. Pour over the beef and pork mixture and toss to coat.

Serve in authentic West Virginia style by arranging the barbecue on the bottom half of a bun, adding coleslaw mixed with mayonnaise-type salad dressing thinned with milk and topping with the bun top.

Serves 6

Polynesian Ribs Exotica

3	to 4 pounds lean beef short ribs	1/3	cup soy sauce
1 1/2	to 2 teaspoons unseasoned meat tenderizer	1/4	cup honey
		1	tablespoon ginger
1	(20-ounce) can pineapple slices	1	tablespoon ketchup
		1/4	teaspoon hot sauce, or to taste

Trim the beef of any excess fat. Cut into serving pieces. Sprinkle with the meat tenderizer. Pierce the beef deeply all over with a fork. Place in a shallow baking dish. Let stand for 30 minutes at room temperature.

Drain the pineapple, reserving 2/3 cup of the syrup. Combine the reserved pineapple syrup, soy sauce, honey, ginger, ketchup and hot sauce in a bowl and mix well. Pour over the beef. Marinate, covered, in the refrigerator for 2 to 3 hours. Drain the beef, reserving the marinade. Boil the reserved marinade in a saucepan for 2 minutes. Remove from the heat.

Place the beef bone side down on a smoker rack. Add dampened hickory to the coals in a smoker. Place the smoker rack over the coals and close the smoker hood. Smoke for 1 3/4 to 2 hours or until the beef is tender, brushing frequently with the reserved marinade. Brush the pineapple with the reserved marinade. Place on the smoker rack with the beef 5 to 10 minutes before the beef is tender. Bring the remaining marinade to a boil and serve with the beef.

Serves 4

Michael Daugherty
Composer-in-Residence

Michael Daugherty, the DSO's Composer-in-Residence, has composed at least one piece of music that would go well with just about any recipe—"Shaken, Not Stirred," a tribute to James Bond, British Agent 007. In a suave succession of timbres and rhythms tinged with cocktail-lounge overtones, the effect of this composition is retro-futuristic music that looks good in a dinner jacket, licensed to thrill. It is scored for electric bass, vibraphone, marimba, and a wide range of percussion instruments, including, of course, crystal martini glasses.

Meats

Beef Stroganoff

2   pounds lean beef, cut into 1-inch squares
1   cup (2 sticks) butter
1   onion, chopped
1   cup sliced mushrooms
1/2 green bell pepper, chopped
1   garlic clove, chopped
1   tablespoon garlic salt
1   tablespoon Worcestershire sauce
    Dash of Tabasco sauce
1   cup sour cream
1   cup heavy cream
3   tablespoons wine vinegar
2   tablespoons flour
2   cups uncooked egg noodles

Sauté the beef in the butter in a skillet until brown. Add the onion, mushrooms, bell pepper, garlic, garlic salt, Worcestershire sauce and Tabasco sauce. Sauté until the vegetables are softened. Add the sour cream, heavy cream and wine vinegar. Stir in the flour. Simmer for 1 hour or until the beef is tender.

Cook the egg noodles using the package directions; drain. Spoon the noodles on a serving platter. Spoon the beef mixture over the hot noodles.

Serves 4

Cranberry Chuck Roast

This is a favorite recipe to prepare in November and December. Serve with mashed potatoes or noodles.

1   (3- to 4-pound) arm or blade chuck pot roast
3   tablespoons shortening or canola oil
1   teaspoon salt
    Pepper to taste
3   tablespoons sugar
1/2 teaspoon cinnamon
1/4 teaspoon ground cloves
2   cups fresh cranberries
1/4 cup hot water

Brown the roast in the shortening in a large ovenproof skillet or Dutch oven; drain. Season the roast with the salt and pepper. Sprinkle with the sugar, cinnamon and cloves. Place 1 cup of the cranberries on top of the roast. Pour 1/4 cup water into the skillet. Cover the skillet tightly. Bake at 300 to 325 degrees for 3 to 3 1/2 hours or until the roast is tender, adding additional hot water if needed. Add the remaining 1 cup cranberries. Bake for 5 to 10 minutes longer or until the cranberries are tender. Remove the roast to a serving platter. Add a small amount of water to the pan drippings. Cook until thickened or until of desired gravy consistency, stirring constantly. Spoon into a gravy boat. Serve with the roast.

Serves 4 to 6

Polish Cabbage Rolls

12   large cabbage leaves
1   egg, beaten
1/4   cup milk
1/4   cup finely chopped onion
      Pinch of salt
1/4   teaspoon pepper
1   pound lean ground beef
1   cup cooked rice
1   (15-ounce) can tomato sauce
1 1/2 cups diced tomatoes
1   tablespoon brown sugar
2   tablespoons lemon juice
2   teaspoons Worcestershire sauce
1/3   cup vegetable broth

Immerse the cabbage leaves in boiling water in a large stockpot and let stand for 3 minutes or until limp; drain. Combine the egg, milk, onion, salt, pepper, ground beef and cooked rice in a large bowl and mix well. Place about 1/4 cup ground beef mixture in the center of each cabbage leaf. Fold in the sides and roll up. Place in a slow cooker. Mix the tomato sauce, tomatoes, brown sugar, lemon juice, Worcestershire sauce and vegetable broth in a bowl. Pour over the cabbage rolls. Cook on Low for 7 to 9 hours or until cooked through.

Serves 6

"Po-Tsarski!"
Bloomfield Hills

The cuisine of the renowned Troika, a favorite restaurant of the Tsars in old St. Petersburg, will be recreated for you in this unique and special luncheon.

Thursday, June 4, 1992
12:30 p.m.

Menu
Zakuski (Hors D'oeuvres)
Baklazhannaya Ikra (Eggplant Caviar)
Syrniki (Cottage Cheese Fritters)
Salat Olivier (Chicken Breast Salad)
Golubtsy (Stuffed Cabbage Rolls) (at left)
Fasol (Kidney Beans)
Salat S Kapustoi (Coleslaw)
Blini (Crepes with Orange Butter and Grand Marnier)
Streudel with Pears and Apples
Lemon Kvas (non-alcoholic drink)
Punsh iz Vina (Wine Punch)

Hosts
Mr. and Mrs. Ramon A. Von Drehle

Music
Ventura String Quartet
Linda Smith, DSO Violin
Marguerite Deslippe, DSO Violin
Hart Hollman, DSO Viola
Mario DiFiore, DSO Violoncello

Motown Strings

In the 1960s, when Berry Gordy was looking to add strings to his new "Motown" sound he turned to the Detroit Symphony Orchestra. Led by concertmaster Gordon Staples, seven members of the string section made frequent after-hours trips to Hitsville, USA, to provide the backup to such songs as, "What's Going On," "Dancing In The Streets," "My Cherie Amour," "My Girl," and a dozen others.

Over the ten years the DSO musicians played for Motown, their parts became more challenging and jazz related. Hearing those songs now brings smiles to the faces of Felix Resnick, Al Score, Bea Staples, and Dave Ireland, violinists still with the Orchestra, who remember "Hitsville, USA" with fondness.

Felix Resnick
DSO violinist since 1942

Easy Sukiyaki

1¹/2   pounds sirloin steak
2   tablespoons vegetable oil
3/4   cup soy sauce
1/4   cup water
1/4   cup sugar
1   medium onion, thinly sliced
1   green bell pepper, cut into strips
3   ribs celery, diagonally sliced
8   ounces fresh mushrooms, sliced
1   (10-ounce) can bamboo shoots, drained
1   small bunch green onions with tops, diagonally sliced
8   cups hot cooked rice (optional)

Cut the steak into 2-inch diagonal slices 1/2 inch thick. Heat the oil in a 10-inch skillet. Add the steak. Cook until light brown. Mix the soy sauce, water and sugar in a small bowl. Add 1/2 of the soy sauce mixture to the skillet. Push the steak to 1 side of the skillet. Add the onion, bell pepper and celery. Cook for 2 minutes. Add the remaining soy sauce mixture, mushrooms and bamboo shoots. Cook for 3 to 5 minutes. Add the green onions. Cook for 1 minute, stirring constantly. Spoon over hot cooked rice.

Serves 8

Meats

Motown Meat Loaf

Meat loaf is the younger cousin of the European pâté, although one would hardly be mistaken for the other. Since the recipe first appeared in print in this country in 1900, meat loaf hasn't been the most popular dish. You rarely hear, "Oh, boy, we're having meat loaf for dinner!" or "Let's send out for some meat loaf." But that's probably because many people, when cooking it, don't give meat loaf the attention it deserves. In order to make it a treat instead of a treatment, meat loaf must be juicy and tasty. Seems basic, but somehow there exists a legacy of dry, tasteless slabs of cooked ground meat. We think this recipe will make you a meat loaf lover. If you like your meat loaf crusty, try brushing some ketchup on the top of the loaf before baking.

Seasoning Mix

2   teaspoons dry mustard
2   teaspoons paprika
1 1/2   teaspoons salt
1 1/2   teaspoons dried thyme leaves
1 1/2   teaspoons dried sweet basil leaves
1   teaspoon garlic powder
1   teaspoon onion powder
1   teaspoon black pepper
1   teaspoon white pepper

Meat Loaf

8   slices bacon, chopped
1 1/2   cups chopped onions
1   cup green bell pepper
1   cup chopped celery
4   bay leaves
3/4   cup tomato juice
1/2   cup evaporated milk
1 1/2   pounds ground beef
8   ounces ground veal
2   eggs, lightly beaten
1/2   cup unsalted saltine crumbs
    (about 12 crackers)

For the seasoning mix, combine all of the seasonings in a bowl and mix well. Store in an airtight container.

For the meat loaf, cook the bacon in a 10-inch skillet over high heat for 7 to 9 minutes or until brown and crispy. Remove the bacon with a slotted spoon to paper towels to drain. Add the onions to the skillet. Cook for 5 to 6 minutes or until the onions are golden brown. Add the bell pepper, celery, bay leaves and 2 tablespoons of the seasoning mix and mix well. Cook for 4 minutes, stirring occasionally. Add the remaining seasoning mix. Cook for 5 to 6 minutes, stirring frequently. Remove from the heat. Remove and discard the bay leaves.

Combine the tomato juice, evaporated milk and cooked bacon in a large bowl. Add the cooked vegetable mixture and mix well.

Mix the ground beef, ground veal, eggs and cracker crumbs in a large bowl. Add the vegetable mixture and mix well, being careful not to pack too tightly. Place in a 9×13-inch baking dish sprayed with nonstick cooking spray. Shape into a thick loaf. Bake at 350 degrees for 30 minutes. Turn the dish a quarter turn. Bake for 15 minutes longer or until cooked through.

Serves 6 to 8

Note: This meat loaf is tender and tends to fall apart easily, which makes it difficult to slice.

Meats

Marinated Ginger Flank Steaks

1/4   *cup vegetable oil*
1/4   *cup soy sauce*
2   *tablespoons wine vinegar*
2   *tablespoons honey*
1/2   *teaspoon ginger*
4   *garlic cloves, minced*
4   *flank steaks, 1 1/2 inches thick*

Mix the oil, soy sauce, wine vinegar, honey, ginger and garlic in a bowl. Place the flank steaks in a sealable plastic food storage bag. Pour the marinade over the steaks and seal the bag. Marinate in the refrigerator for 24 hours.

Drain the steaks, discarding the marinade. Arrange the steaks on a rack in a broiler pan. Broil until the desired degree of doneness. Slice the steak at an angle to serve.

Serves 4

Veal Scaloppine with Marsala

1   *pound boneless veal*
3   *tablespoons flour*
     Pepper to taste
1/4   *cup (1/2 stick) butter*
8   *ounces fresh mushrooms, sliced*
2   *tablespoons beef bouillon*
1/2   *cup dry marsala*
     Sprigs of fresh parsley

Place the veal between 2 sheets of waxed pepper. Pound until thin. Cut into thin serving pieces. Mix the flour and pepper in a bowl. Add the veal and coat well. Heat the butter in a skillet until sizzling. Add the veal. Cook over high heat until brown on both sides. Add the mushrooms. Sauté briefly. Add the beef bouillon and wine. Sauté for 1 minute. Arrange the veal on a serving platter. Pour the pan juices over the top. Garnish with fresh parsley sprigs.

Serves 4

Saltimbocca alla Romana

12	thinly sliced veal medallions
	Salt and pepper to taste
	Flour
12	fresh sage leaves, cut into halves
12	thin slices prosciutto
6	tablespoons unsalted butter
1	cup pale dry sherry
2	tablespoons unsalted butter

Season the veal with salt and pepper. Sprinkle with flour. Place sage and prosciutto on each slice and secure with a wooden pick.

Melt 6 tablespoons butter in a skillet over high heat. Add the veal. Sauté until brown and cooked through. Remove the veal to a heated platter.

Add the wine to the skillet, stirring to deglaze. Cook until the mixture is reduced by 1/3. Add 2 tablespoons butter. Return the veal to the skillet and coat with the sauce. Cook until heated through.

Serves 6

Glories of the Tuscan Table
Grosse Pointe Farms

Journey to Tuscany, birthplace of two of history's most glorious achievements—the Renaissance and Tuscan cuisine.

Saturday, August 21, 1993
6:30 p.m.

Menu
First Course
Agnolotti alla Piemontese, con Panna—
Agnolotti with Cream, Piemontese Style
Insalata Mista All' Italiana, Aceto Balsamico—
Salad of Mixed Greens, Balsamic Vinegar Dressing
Entrée
Involtini Da Edoardo, Funghi Freschi—
Veal Bundles Filled with Spinach, Prosciutto, and Fontina Cheese, Sherry and Wine Sauce,
Fresh Mushrooms
Dessert
Torta Toscanella, Chantilly Cream

Appropriate Wines

Hosts
Dr. and Mrs. Frank Nesi

Music
Kim Minasian Hawes, Soprano
Margaret Hall, Mezzo-Soprano
Mark Vondrak, Baritone

Wine
Compliments of Mr. and Mrs. James Lutfy,
Cloverleaf Market

Food
Compliments of Da Edoardo Restaurant

Flowers
Compliments of Conner Park Florist

A Provence Lunch
Bloomfield Hills

Celebrate Bastille Day with a French countryside bistro luncheon served on the authentic linens that characterize Provence. Enjoy this feast prepared with love and skill and savor the succulent tastes that have made French cuisine a legend.
Vive la France!

Menu
Portobello Salad with
Whole Grain Mustard Vinaigrette
Shrimp Bisque
Veal Madeira (at right) with Potatoes Boulangère
and Ratatouille
Cherry Bread Pudding
Coffee and Tea
Wines will be selected to complement the menu

Friday, July 14, 2000
Noon

Your Host
Jean Carman

Catering
Brandy's

Wines
Courtesy of Elie Wines

Musical Performance
The De Villen Quartet
Philip Dikeman, Flute
Laura Rowe, Violin
Caroline Coade, Viola
Alicia Rowe, Cello

Veal Madeira Scaloppine

1/2	cup flour
	Salt and pepper to taste
2	tablespoons margarine
6	(2-ounce) slices veal scaloppine
1	garlic clove, minced
1/2	shallot, minced
4	mushroom caps, thinly sliced
1/3	cup madeira
1	teaspoon tomato paste
2/3	cup demi-glace
	Chopped fresh parsley or sliced scallions

Mix the flour, salt and pepper in a shallow dish. Melt the margarine in a large sauté pan. Dredge the veal in the flour mixture. Add to the hot margarine in the pan. Cook for 2 minutes or until brown and turn. Add the garlic, shallot and mushrooms. Sauté for 2 minutes. Add the wine. Cook for 15 seconds or until the liquid is reduced. Add the tomato paste and demi-glace. Simmer for 3 minutes. Spoon onto a serving platter. Garnish with chopped fresh parsley or sliced scallions.

Serves 2

Meats

"Red-eye" Braised Lamb Shanks and Beans

6   (1-pound each) lamb shanks
    Salt to taste
3   tablespoons vegetable oil
1   pound dried kidney beans (about 2¹/4 cups)
1   large onion, finely chopped
1   red bell pepper, finely chopped
1   large carrot, cut into ¹/4-inch pieces
4   garlic cloves, chopped
2   bacon slices, chopped
4   cups water
2   cups brewed coffee
    Bouquet garni of 5 sprigs of fresh parsley, 3 sprigs
        of fresh thyme and 2 sprigs of fresh rosemary
2   bay leaves
¹/2   teaspoon hot red pepper flakes

Pat the lamb shanks dry. Season with salt to taste. Heat the oil in a heavy ovenproof stockpot until hot but not smoking. Brown the shanks in 2 batches in the hot oil, removing to a heated platter after each batch. Rinse and sort the beans. Add the beans to the stockpot. Place the shanks on top of the beans in a single layer. Add the onion, bell pepper, carrot, garlic, bacon, water, coffee, bouquet garni, bay leaves and red pepper flakes. Bring to a boil over high heat. Do not stir. Cover tightly and place on the middle oven rack. Bake at 300 degrees for 3 hours or until the lamb and beans are tender.

Remove the lamb and beans to a heated platter using a slotted spoon. Discard the bouquet garni and bay leaves. Boil the braising liquid for 5 minutes or until slightly thickened. Pour over the shanks and beans.

Serves 6

Roast Rack of Lamb Persillade

¹/2   cup olive oil
5   to 6 garlic cloves, sliced
1   tablespoon cracked pepper
2   sprigs of fresh rosemary
    French rack of lamb
    Honeycup mustard
1   cup fresh white bread crumbs
1   tablespoon chopped fresh basil
1   tablespoon chopped fresh thyme
1   teaspoon chopped fresh rosemary
    Salt and pepper to taste
    Olive oil

Combine ¹/2 cup olive oil, garlic, cracked pepper and rosemary sprigs in a bowl and mix well. Pour over the lamb in a shallow dish. Marinate, covered, in the refrigerator for 2 to 12 hours. Drain the lamb, discarding the marinade. Place in a hot skillet. Pan-sear until golden brown. Remove to a baking sheet. Coat the lamb with Honeycup mustard.

Combine the bread crumbs, basil, thyme, chopped rosemary, salt and pepper to taste in a bowl and mix well. Add enough olive oil to lightly coat the bread crumbs. Press over the lamb. Bake at 300 degrees for 10 to 20 minutes or until medium-rare. Remove from the oven. Let stand for 10 minutes before slicing.

Serves 2

Meats

Ham Loaves

This is a great way to use leftover Christmas or Easter hams. Serve hot or cold with the sauce.

Ham Loaves

2   pounds lean smoked ham, ground
2   pounds lean fresh pork, ground
1¹/2   cups fresh cracker crumbs
¹/3   cup chopped onion
4   eggs, beaten
1¹/4   teaspoons salt
2   cups milk
2   tablespoons chopped parsley

Ham Glaze

1   cup plus 2 tablespoons packed brown sugar
     (8 ounces)
¹/2   cup cider vinegar
1¹/2   tablespoons dry mustard

Zippy Sauce

¹/2   cup sour cream
¹/2   cup mayonnaise
¹/4   cup prepared mustard
2   tablespoons prepared horseradish
1   tablespoon minced chives
     Salt to taste
     Lemon juice to taste

For the ham loaves, mix the ham, pork and crackers in a large bowl. Add the onion, eggs, salt, milk and parsley and mix well. Shape into 2 loaves. Place in two 5×9-inch loaf pans. Bake at 350 degrees for 30 minutes.

For the glaze, combine the brown sugar, vinegar and dry mustard in a saucepan. Bring to a boil. Boil for 1 minute, stirring constantly.

Remove the loaves from the oven. Baste with the glaze. Place on a baking sheet to catch the drippings. Bake for 1 hour. Cool slightly. Remove the loaves from the pans while still warm.

For the sauce, combine the sour cream, mayonnaise, prepared mustard, prepared horseradish, chives, salt and lemon juice in a bowl and mix well.

To serve, cut the ham loaves into slices and serve with the sauce.

Makes 2 loaves

Note: You may wrap the cooled loaves and freeze. Remove from the freezer 1¹/2 hours before serving if you are serving cold, or sooner if you wish to reheat. Reheat by baking at 325 degrees for 20 minutes. The Zippy Sauce should not be frozen.

Transylvanian Baked Sauerkraut and Pork

Wondrous legends and fabulous food originate from Transylvania. This hearty casserole has many versions, but sauerkraut and pork are always the main ingredients. The secret to its success is that quintessential of Hungarian spices, paprika. It should be imported from Hungary and should be relatively fresh, aromatic, and sweet. It is available in many of our fine local supermarkets. The pork need not be totally lean, because after cooking and shredding it may become too dry. This dish can be served as a main course with some good bread or rolls, preceeded by soup and followed with a light dessert. Serve with a dry red wine or beer. It can also be served as a first course or at a buffet table. It freezes well and is even better reheated.

2	medium onions, chopped		Pinch of cayenne pepper
3	tablespoons vegetable oil	1/2	cup water
2	teaspoons paprika	1/2	cup uncooked rice, cooked
2 1/2	pounds pork stew	1	(40-ounce) package
2	teaspoons paprika		sauerkraut, drained
1	teaspoon salt	1 1/2	cups sour cream
1/2	teaspoon black pepper	6	slices bacon, partially cooked

Sauté the onions in the oil in a skillet over medium heat until translucent. Stir in 2 teaspoons paprika. Increase the heat. Add the pork. Cook until brown, stirring frequently. Add 2 teaspoons paprika, salt, black pepper, cayenne pepper and water. Reduce the heat. Cook for 1 1/2 to 2 hours or until the pork is tender. Remove from the heat. Cool slightly. Shred the pork in a food processor. Do not overprocess. Mix the pork and rice in a bowl. Arrange a thin layer of sauerkraut in an 8×12-inch baking dish. Drop spoonfuls of the pork mixture over the sauerkraut, patting evenly to cover the sauerkraut completely. Spread with a generous layer of the sour cream. Continue alternating the layers with the remaining sauerkraut, pork mixture and sour cream, ending with the sauerkraut and being careful not to mix the sauerkraut with the sour cream beneath. Arrange the partially cooked bacon over the top. Bake at 350 degrees for 30 minutes.

Serves 6 to 8

Family Ties
Beatriz Budinszky Staples
Greg Staples

There are many interesting stories to be found in a symphony orchestra, and the DSO is no exception. How many orchestras can boast of having a mother and son as members? Violinists Beatriz Budinszky Staples and her son Greg Staples form that unique combination. It is a dream come true for the son of the late Gordon Staples, DSO concertmaster for twenty years. Auditioning along with over one hundred other violinists to win his position, Greg now shares the stage with his mother and follows in his father's footsteps. An added bonus for Greg is the opportunity to enjoy, quite often, his mother's excellent Hungarian cooking, such as Transylvanian Baked Sauerkraut and Pork.

Meats

Pork Chop and Potato Bake

4   thick pork chops
    Salt and pepper to taste
1   tablespoon butter
1   large onion, cut into slices, separated into rings
4   boiled potatoes, cut into quarters
1   tablespoon flour
1/2 cup stock or water
1   teaspoon vinegar
1   cup sour cream
    Dash of garlic salt

Brown the pork chops in a dry hot skillet. Season with salt and pepper. Arrange the pork chops in a large baking dish. Add the butter and onion to the skillet. Cook until the onion is translucent. Arrange the potatoes between the pork chops. Drain the onion, reserving the drippings in the skillet. Arrange the onion over the pork chops. Stir the flour into the reserved drippings in the skillet. Add the stock and vinegar. Cook until thickened, stirring constantly. Stir in the sour cream and garlic salt. Pour over the pork chops. Bake, covered, at 375 degrees for 30 minutes. Bake, uncovered, for 30 minutes longer.

Serves 4

Chinese-Style Pork Spareribs

1   side of pork spareribs
2   tablespoons soy sauce
1/3 cup hoisin sauce
1/3 cup ketchup

Marinate the pork in the soy sauce in a shallow dish for 20 minutes or longer, basting frequently. Place the pork in a baking dish. Mix the hoisin sauce and ketchup in a bowl. Brush the pork with the hoisin sauce mixture, coating completely. Bake at 450 degrees for 45 to 55 minutes or until cooked through and brown.

Serves 2

Pork Spareribs with Horseradish Sauce

2   tablespoons prepared horseradish
1   teaspoon dry mustard
1   (14-ounce) bottle ketchup
2   tablespoons chopped green bell pepper
2   tablespoons chopped onion
2   cups water
2 1/2 pounds pork spareribs, browned, drained

Combine the horseradish, dry mustard, ketchup, bell pepper, onion and water in a saucepan. Bring to a boil. Place the drained pork in a baking dish. Pour the boiling sauce over the pork. Bake at 350 to 375 degrees for 1 1/2 hours or until tender and cooked through.

Serves 4

Lapin Sauce Moutarde

Delicious served with mashed potatoes or hot cooked rice.

1	*rabbit, dressed*
	Dijon mustard
3	*tablespoons unsalted butter*
1	*tablespoon canola oil*
1	*bottle dry white wine*
2	*cups chopped shallots*
1	*tablespoon dried herbes de Provence*

Cut the rabbit into serving pieces. Rub each piece with Dijon mustard. Melt the butter with the canola oil in a skillet over medium heat. Add the prepared rabbit. Cook until brown. Remove to a platter and keep warm.

Pour 1/2 cup of the wine into the skillet. Cook over medium heat, stirring to deglaze the skillet. Add the shallots. Cook until golden brown. Return the rabbit to the skillet. Add the herbes de Provence and remaining wine. Increase the heat to high and bring to a boil. Reduce the heat to medium-low. Simmer for 1 hour or until cooked through.

Serves 4

Poultry

Poultry

Chicken Paprikash with Homemade Noodles

Chicken Paprikash

1   (3- to 4-pound) chicken
1   to 1 1/2 cups chopped sweet onions
1   to 2 tablespoons vegetable oil
1/2   red or green bell pepper, chopped
2   tablespoons sweet Hungarian paprika
1/2   teaspoon hot Hungarian paprika, or to taste
1/2   cup (about) water
1   to 2 tablespoons flour
3/4   cup sour cream

Homemade Noodles

1/2   cup flour
1   extra-large egg
Cold water
Melted butter

For the chicken paprikash, cut the chicken into pieces, reserving the back and rib cage for another purpose. Sauté the onions in the oil in a skillet until transparent. Add the bell pepper. Sauté until the bell pepper is slightly softened. Add the sweet and hot paprika and sauté lightly, being sure not to scorch. Add 1/2 cup water and chicken pieces. Cook over very low heat until the chicken is cooked through.

Mix the flour with a small amount of cold water in a bowl to form a smooth paste. Add the sour cream and mix well. Add some of the hot chicken stock and mix well. Add to the skillet. Cook for 3 to 4 minutes or until thickened, stirring constantly.

For the noodles, mix the flour and egg in a bowl. Add enough cold water to make a very soft and sticky dough. Drop by teaspoonfuls into rapidly boiling water in a saucepan. Cook for 2 to 3 minutes or until the noodles are tender.

To serve, drain the noodles and toss with melted butter. Place on a serving platter. Spoon the chicken paprikash over the top.

Serves 4

Note: You may make as many noodles as you desire by using 1 extra-large egg for each 1/2 cup flour.

98

Barbecued Chicken

1¹/2 cups water
1¹/2 cups ketchup
6   tablespoons lemon juice
¹/4   cup Worcestershire sauce
3   tablespoons cider vinegar
3   tablespoons light brown sugar
1   tablespoon prepared mustard
1   teaspoon salt
4   drops of Tabasco sauce, or to taste
1   cup thinly sliced celery
2   tablespoons olive oil
2   tablespoons butter
1   (3- to 3¹/2-pound) chicken
1   cup chopped onion

Mix the water, ketchup, lemon juice, Worcestershire sauce, vinegar, brown sugar, mustard, salt and Tabasco sauce in a bowl. Stir in the celery.

Heat the olive oil and butter in a skillet. Add the chicken. Cook until the chicken is brown. Remove the chicken to a roasting pan. Add the onion to the drippings in the skillet. Cook until the onion is brown, stirring to deglaze the skillet. Add the celery mixture. Simmer for 30 minutes, stirring occasionally. Pour over the chicken. Bake, covered, at 325 to 350 degrees for 1 hour. Bake, uncovered, for 20 to 30 minutes longer or until the chicken is cooked through and the sauce is thickened.

Serves 4 to 6

*Note: You may use selected pieces of chicken,
such as legs or thighs.*

Johannes Brahms
German Composer
(1833–1897)

Brahms, who enjoyed his food, was distressed when he became ill and his doctor prescribed a strict diet.

"But this evening I am dining with Strauss and we shall have chicken paprika," he protested. "Out of the question," said the doctor. "Very well then," said Brahams. "Please consider that I did not come to consult with you until tomorrow."

Poultry

Hoisin Shoyu Chicken

3/4   cup shoyu (soy sauce)
1/4   cup hoisin sauce
1/4   cup sherry
3   tablespoons honey
1/2   cup packed brown sugar
2   cups water
5   tablespoons chopped ginger
6   garlic cloves, crushed
1   cup minced green onions
5   pounds skinless chicken thighs
5   tablespoons cornstarch
1/2   cup cold water
2   tablespoons Chinese parsley

Combine the shoyu, hoisin sauce, sherry, honey, brown sugar, 2 cups water, ginger, garlic and green onions in a large saucepan. Bring to a boil. Add the chicken. Cook, covered, over medium heat for 35 to 40 minutes or until tender. Mix the cornstarch and 1/2 cup cold water in a bowl. Add to the chicken mixture. Cook for 2 to 3 minutes or until thickened, stirring constantly. Sprinkle with Chinese parsley.

Serves 6 to 8

Chicken en Croûte

8   ounces mushrooms
3   shallots
     Salt and pepper to taste
6   (6- to 8-ounce) boneless skinless chicken breasts
     Butter
1   (17-ounce) package frozen puff pastry, thawed
1   (10-ounce) can cream of chicken soup
     Egg whites, lightly beaten

Grind the mushrooms and shallots and place in a skillet. Cook over low heat until the moisture evaporates. Season with salt and pepper. Sear the chicken breasts in hot melted butter in a skillet. Remove from the heat to cool. Unfold the puff pastry on a lightly floured surface. Cut into 6 large squares. Spoon a heaping tablespoon of soup on 1/2 of each square. Arrange a chicken breast over the soup in each square. Spoon the mushroom mixture on top of the chicken. Fold each puff pastry over the chicken and press the edges to seal and enclose the chicken. Arrange on a nonstick baking sheet. Brush with egg whites and pierce with a fork. Bake at 350 to 400 degrees for 20 minutes or until cooked through and golden brown.

Serves 6

Note: You may assemble a day ahead and chill, wrapped, in the refrigerator. Bake just before serving.

Spicy Oven-Fried Chicken

4	cups wheat flakes or corn flakes, lightly crushed	1	teaspoon paprika
1	garlic clove, crushed, or 1/2 teaspoon minced garlic (optional)	1/4	teaspoon salt (optional) Freshly ground pepper to taste
1	teaspoon ground ginger	12	skinless chicken pieces (3 1/2 pounds)

Mix the wheat flake crumbs and garlic on a piece of foil. Combine the ginger, paprika, salt and pepper in a small bowl and mix well. Coat the chicken with the ginger mixture. Roll in the crumb mixture to coat. Spray lightly with butter-flavor nonstick cooking spray. Arrange on a baking sheet sprayed with butter-flavor nonstick cooking spray. Bake at 350 degrees for 45 to 60 minutes or until golden brown and cooked through.

Serves 6

Balsamic Chicken

4	skinless chicken breasts	1/4	cup balsamic vinegar
2	tablespoons flour	3/4	cup chicken broth
	Salt and pepper to taste	1	bay leaf
	Garlic clove slices to taste	1/2	teaspoon fresh thyme, or 1/4 teaspoon dried thyme
2	tablespoons olive oil		
12	ounces whole mushrooms		

Coat the chicken in a mixture of flour, salt and pepper. Heat the garlic in the olive oil in a large skillet. Add the chicken. Cook until the chicken is light brown. Add the mushrooms. Cook for 3 minutes. Add the balsamic vinegar, chicken broth, bay leaf and thyme. Cook, covered, over medium heat for 10 minutes or until the chicken is cooked through, turning the chicken occasionally. Discard the bay leaf. Serve with noodles or hot cooked rice.

Serves 4

While in Japan with the DSO in 1998, Jill Woodward (Director of Public Relations) went with a group of musicians to an historic village near Toyota City. In addition to historic exhibits, there were food booths. She was enthusiastic when she thought she saw something that looked like Thai satay, generally chicken on a skewer. She was less enthusiastic when she learned it was really sparrow—feet still attached—on the skewer. Orchestra Fellow Derek Reeves tried one and ate the whole thing! He thought it was "interesting."

Poultry

Curried Chicken Broccoli Casserole

4   boneless skinless chicken breasts
    Salt and pepper to taste
1   bunch broccoli, cut into pieces
1   (10-ounce) can cream of chicken soup
1/4 cup mayonnaise-type salad dressing
3/4 to 1 teaspoon curry powder
2   tablespoons white wine
1   cup shredded Havarti cheese
    Croutons
    Paprika to taste

Arrange the chicken in a baking dish. Sprinkle with salt and pepper. Bake at 350 degrees until the chicken is tender. Drain the chicken, reserving the pan drippings.

Cook the broccoli in a small amount of water in a saucepan until tender; drain.

Combine the soup, mayonnaise-type salad dressing, curry powder, wine and a small amount of the reserved drippings in a bowl and mix well.

To assemble, place the broccoli in a 7×11-inch glass baking dish. Layer the chicken over the broccoli. Pour the soup mixture over the layers. Sprinkle with the cheese, croutons and paprika. Bake at 350 degrees for 45 minutes.

Serves 4

Light and Zesty Chicken and Rice

4   chicken breasts
1/3 cup Italian salad dressing
2/3 cup uncooked rice
1   (16-ounce) package frozen broccoli, carrots and water chestnuts
1   (2-ounce) can French-fried onions
13/4 cups chicken bouillon
1/2 teaspoon Italian seasoning

Place the chicken in an 8×12-inch baking dish. Pour the salad dressing over the chicken. Bake, uncovered, at 400 degrees for 20 minutes. Place the rice, vegetable mixture and 1/2 of the French-fried onions around the chicken. Add the bouillon. Sprinkle with the Italian seasoning. Bake, uncovered, at 400 degrees for 25 minutes. Top with the remaining 1/2 can French-fried onions. Bake for 2 to 3 minutes longer. Let stand for 5 minutes before serving.

Serves 4 to 6

Note: To prepare in the microwave, place the rice and bouillon in a microwave-safe dish. Microwave, covered, on High for 5 minutes. Stir in the vegetable mixture and 1/2 of the French-fried onions, salad dressing and Italian seasoning. Arrange the chicken over the mixture. Microwave, covered, on Medium for 15 to 17 minutes. Top with the remaining French-fried onions. Microwave, uncovered, for 1 minute. Let stand for 5 minutes before serving.

Chicken Jacque

1 1/2   pounds boneless skinless chicken breasts
19   ounces cream cheese, softened
4   garlic cloves, chopped
1 1/2   green bell peppers, chopped
1   green onion, finely chopped
12   ounces mushrooms, chopped
1/2   cup (1 stick) butter
1   tablespoon chicken base or bouillon
1   tablespoon milk
1   tablespoon seasoned salt
        Salt and pepper to taste
1   egg
1/2   cup milk
1   (17-ounce) package puff pastry

Boil the chicken in water to cover in a saucepan for 40 minutes or until the chicken is cooked through; drain. Chop into medium pieces. Sauté the garlic, bell peppers, green onion and mushrooms in the butter in a skillet. Combine the chicken, cream cheese, sautéed vegetables, chicken base and 1 tablespoon milk in a large bowl and mix well using your hands. Season with seasoned salt, salt and pepper.

Beat the egg and milk in a bowl. Unfold the puff pastry sheets on a lightly floured surface. Roll each into a 12×12-inch square. Cut each square into 4-inch squares. Spoon the chicken mixture onto each square. Brush the edges of each square with the egg mixture. Fold each puff pastry into a triangle, pressing the edges together to enclose the filling. Place on a nonstick baking sheet. Bake at 350 degrees for 30 minutes or until golden brown.

Serves 8

An Intimate Dinner for Eight
Dearborn

The menu says it all! Bon appétit!

Menu
Champagne
Wrede's Grilled Pizza with Grapes and Soppressata
Chicken Jacque (at left)
Maryland Crab Cakes
Salmon Gravlax
Fruit Kabobs
Chicken Consommé with Jardinière Spring Vegetables
Black Sea Bass with Somen Noodles
Leafy Spring Spinach Greens with Fresh Strawberries,
Mandarin Oranges
Michigan Dried Cherries
Raspberry Vinaigrette Dressing
Veal Chop with Sorrel, Tasso and Foie Gras
Roasted Parisienne Potatoes
Fresh Asparagus Tips and Baby Carrots
Le Grand Gâteau Crème de Passion with
Mango Grande Passion Sauce
Coffee and Tea
Wines will be selected to complement the menu

Saturday, May 19, 2001
7:00 p.m.

Your Hosts
Gloria and Stan Nycek

Catering
Chef Richard Teeple
Henry Ford Community College

Wine
Courtesy of John Jonna, Merchant's Fine Wine

Musical Performance
Lyric Piano Trio
Pat Daoust, Piano
Kathy Zuchniewicz, Violin
Eleanore Smith, Cello

Poultry

Marinated Chicken

2   pounds boneless skinless chicken breasts
1/4 cup soy sauce
2   tablespoons peach or apple juice
1   tablespoon orange juice
1   teaspoon brown sugar
1   tablespoon chopped chives
2   to 3 tablespoons olive oil
1   small garlic clove, thinly sliced
2   teaspoons honey
1/4 teaspoon ginger
1   teaspoon red wine vinegar

Arrange the chicken in a shallow baking dish. Combine the soy sauce, peach juice, orange juice, brown sugar, chives, olive oil, garlic, honey, ginger and red wine vinegar in a bowl and mix well. Pour over the chicken. Marinate, covered, in the refrigerator for 1 1/2 hours, turning once or twice. Remove from the refrigerator. Marinate at room temperature for 30 minutes. Bake, uncovered, at 375 degrees for 40 minutes and turn the chicken. Bake, covered, for 15 to 20 minutes longer or until the chicken is cooked through. Remove the chicken to a heated platter, reserving the marinade. Cook the reserved marinade in a saucepan until reduced to the desired consistency. Serve the chicken with the reduced marinade and hot cooked rice.

Serves 4 to 6

Greek Lemon Chicken

4   skinless chicken breasts
4   baking potatoes, peeled, cut into 1×2-inch pieces
1/2 tablespoon oregano
     Garlic powder, salt and pepper to taste
     Juice of 1 lemon
1/2 tablespoon oregano
1   cup olive oil
     Juice of 1/2 lemon

Arrange the chicken in a large nonstick roasting pan. Add the potatoes. Sprinkle with 1/2 tablespoon oregano, garlic powder, salt and pepper. Drizzle with the juice of 1 lemon. Toss the chicken mixture with your hands to evenly distribute the seasonings. Sprinkle with 1/2 tablespoon oregano. Add 1/2 cup of the olive oil.

Preheat the oven to 450 degrees. Reduce the oven temperature to 325 degrees. Place the chicken on the middle oven rack. Bake for 35 minutes. Turn the chicken and potatoes. Add the remaining olive oil and sprinkle with the juice of 1/2 lemon. Bake for 35 minutes or until cooked through.

Arrange the chicken and potatoes on a serving platter. Pour the pan drippings over the top.

Serves 4

Honey Pecan Chicken

4	ounces pecans, chopped	1	small jar honey
2	tablespoons Grey Poupon mustard	1	small jar creamy honey mustard
6	boneless skinless chicken breasts	2	tablespoons half-and-half

Mix the pecans and Grey Poupon mustard in a bowl. Dip the chicken in the honey in a bowl. Press the pecan mixture over both sides of the chicken to coat. Arrange in a glass 9×12-inch baking dish. Bake, uncovered, at 375 degrees for 35 minutes.

Combine the honey mustard and half-and-half in a saucepan. Cook over low heat until heated through. Drizzle over the chicken before serving. Serve with the remaining honey mustard mixture.

Serves 6

Chicken Gabrielle

1	pound broccoli or asparagus, cooked	1	teaspoon curry powder
3	pounds boneless skinless chicken, cooked, chopped	4	drops of Tabasco sauce
3	cups canned cream of mushroom soup	1	tablespoon chopped pimentos
1	cup cream	1/4	cup grated Parmesan cheese Paprika to taste

Arrange the broccoli in a greased 9×13-inch baking dish. Arrange the chicken over the broccoli. Combine the soup, cream, curry powder and Tabasco sauce in a saucepan and mix well. Cook over low heat until smooth, stirring constantly. Stir in the pimentos. Pour over the chicken. Sprinkle with the Parmesan cheese and paprika. Bake at 400 degrees for 15 minutes.

Serves 8

The late Lyell Lindsey, Detroit native and DSO bassoonist and contra-bassoonist from 1962 to 1991, possessed a sense of humor well known to his musician colleagues. In the early 1970s, during the DSO's Ford Auditorium years, a young musician new to the orchestra asked Lyell if a nearby greasy-spoon tavern would be acceptable for lunch during the one-hour break between rehearsals. Lyell answered, "The Carry-On Tavern? Sure. Choose what you want from the menu and when you get your order, take a big bite and chew it and enjoy it. Just make sure you don't swallow." (Note: The name of the tavern has been changed, even though it has been gone for years.)

Poultry

Chicken Pie

1   unbaked (2-crust) pie pastry
2   cups chopped cooked chicken
1   tablespoon flour
1   cup chopped carrots
1   cup chopped onion
1/4   cup chopped celery
1/8   teaspoon pepper
1/4   cup (1/2 stick) butter
1   (10-ounce) can cream of chicken soup
1   cup cooked cut green beans

Line a 9-inch pie plate with 1/2 of the pastry. Toss the chicken with the flour in a bowl. Sauté the carrots, onion, celery and pepper in the butter in a skillet until tender. Stir in the soup, chicken mixture and green beans. Pour into the pastry-lined pie plate.

Roll out the remaining pastry on a lightly floured surface. Cut into 1/2-inch strips. Arrange the strips over the pie to form a lattice top, sealing and fluting the edge. Bake at 350 degrees for 45 minutes or until the crust is golden brown.

Serves 6

Note: You may also use turkey instead of the chicken.

Spicy Garlic Chicken Pizza

12   ounces boneless skinless chicken breasts
1/4   cup sliced green onions
2   garlic cloves, minced
2   tablespoons rice vinegar or white vinegar
2   tablespoons reduced-sodium soy sauce
1   tablespoon olive oil or vegetable oil
1/2   teaspoon crushed red pepper, or 1/4 teaspoon
      ground red pepper
1/4   teaspoon black pepper
1   tablespoon cornstarch
1   tablespoon olive oil or vegetable oil
1   (12-inch) Boboli bread shell
1/2   cup shredded Monterey Jack cheese
1/2   cup shredded mozzarella cheese
1/4   cup sliced green onions
2   tablespoons pine nuts or sliced almonds

Cut the chicken into 1/2-inch pieces. Combine 1/4 cup green onions, garlic, vinegar, soy sauce, 1 tablespoon olive oil, red pepper and black pepper in a bowl and mix well. Add the chicken and stir to coat. Marinate at room temperature for 30 minutes. Drain the chicken, reserving the marinade. Mix the reserved marinade and cornstarch in a bowl.

Sauté the chicken in 1 tablespoon olive oil in a skillet for 3 minutes or until cooked through. Add the reserved marinade mixture. Cook until thickened and bubbly, stirring constantly. Spoon evenly over the bread shell. Sprinkle with Monterey Jack cheese and mozzarella cheese. Bake, uncovered, at 400 degrees for 12 minutes. Sprinkle with 1/4 cup green onions and pine nuts. Bake for 2 minutes.

Serves 6

Turkey Tortilla Casserole

A great way to enjoy leftover turkey.

4	to 5 cups chopped cooked turkey or chicken
2	(10-ounce) cans cream of mushroom soup
2	(4-ounce) cans chopped green chiles
2	(7-ounce) cans green chile salsa
2	(2-ounce) cans sliced black olives, drained
2/3	cup thinly sliced green onions
3/4	teaspoon cumin
8	corn tortillas, cut into 1/2-inch strips
2	cups shredded Monterey Jack cheese
2	cups shredded Cheddar cheese

Combine the turkey, soup, chiles, salsa, black olives, green onions and cumin in a bowl and mix well. Arrange 1/2 of the tortilla strips in a greased shallow 3-quart baking dish. Layer 1/2 of the turkey mixture, Monterey Jack cheese, remaining tortilla strips and remaining turkey mixture in the prepared dish. Sprinkle with the Cheddar cheese. Chill, covered, for up to 24 hours if desired. Bake, uncovered, at 350 degrees for 30 to 45 minutes or until heated through and bubbly. Let stand for 5 minutes before serving.

Serves 6 to 8

Arturo Toscanini
Italian Conductor
(1867–1957)

Arriving at a town on July 3 during a South American tour with the NBC Symphony Orchestra, Toscanini told the disgruntled players that he wished them to assemble at the theater the following morning. The players, who had been traveling for some time, were looking forward to a couple of days' rest from rehearsals. They obeyed with an ill grace. When they were assembled, Toscanini asked them to rise and led them through "The Star-Spangled Banner." "Today is the Fourth of July," he announced at the end, and dismissed them.

Poultry

Ursula's Turkey Meat Loaf

3   pounds ground turkey
2   eggs, beaten
2   cups sliced onions
2   cups sliced carrots
2¹/2 cups chopped portobello mushrooms
4   cups broccoli florets
     Minced garlic to taste
     Salt and pepper to taste
3/4 cup The Jug barbecue sauce

Combine the ground turkey and eggs in a bowl and mix lightly with a fork. Add the onions, carrots, mushrooms, broccoli, garlic, salt, pepper and barbecue sauce and mix well. Shape into a loaf and place in a 5×7-inch glass baking dish. Bake at 400 degrees for 1 hour or until cooked through.

Serves 8

Duck with Cranberry Orange Glaze

Duck

6   (8-ounce) duck breasts
     Salt and pepper to taste

Cranberry Orange Glaze

1   cup cranberries
1/3 cup orange juice
1/2 cup orange marmalade
2   ounces bourbon
1/4 teaspoon thyme
     Salt and pepper to taste
2   tablespoons butter, chilled (optional)

For the duck, trim the skin to the shape of the duck breasts. Score the skin in 1/4-inch intervals. Rotate the duck and score again to make a criss-cross pattern. Season with salt and pepper. Cook the duck in a nonstick skillet over low to medium-low heat for 8 to 12 minutes or until the fat is rendered and the skin is crisp and brown. Turn the duck. Cook for 1 to 2 minutes longer. Arrange the duck on a baking sheet. Bake at 325 degrees for 3 to 4 minutes or until a meat thermometer inserted into the thickest portion registers 160 degrees. Let stand for 2 to 3 minutes.

For the glaze, combine the cranberries, orange juice, orange marmalade, bourbon and thyme in a medium saucepan. Bring to a boil and reduce the heat. Simmer for 10 minutes, stirring occasionally. Season with salt and pepper. Remove from the heat. Add the butter for a richer sauce and whisk until melted.

To serve, slice the duck into medallions. Place on serving plates. Spoon the glaze over each medallion.

Serves 6

Curried Duck Salad

2	roasted ducks
1	cup mayonnaise
2/3	cup chutney, puréed
2²/3	tablespoons curry powder
2¹/2	teaspoons lemon juice
2²/3	tablespoons honey
1	teaspoon white vinegar
2	large ribs celery, finely chopped
1	small onion, finely chopped
2	apples, chopped
1/4	cup toasted sliced almonds
	Salt and pepper to taste

Chop the ducks, discarding the skin and bones. Combine the mayonnaise, chutney, curry powder, lemon juice, honey and vinegar in a bowl and mix well. Add the chicken, celery, onion, apples and almonds and toss to mix well. Season with salt and pepper. Chill, covered, for 2 hours or longer before serving.

Serves 8

Ouvertures et Finales
Bingham Farms

Experience a harmonious blend of food, music, and art in a unique architectural setting.

Saturday, August 1, 1992
6:30 p.m.

Menu
Hors d'oeuvres
Caviar Roulade
Mousse de Fruits de Mer
Salade de Canard
Paté Volaille
Jambon Persille
Quelques Autres Choses
Les Desserts Assorties
Chocolat Intemperance
Roulade Noisettes
Gâteau de Fraises
Gâteau au Fromage de citron

Sparkling and Dessert Wines

Hosts
Mr. and Mrs. William Bostick
Miss Katherine Wasserfallen

Music
Marguerite Deslippe, DSO Violin
James Waring, DSO Violin
Glenn Mellow, DSO Viola
Mario DiFiore, DSO Violoncello
Maxim Janowsky, DSO Bass

Flowers
Compliments of The Orchid Garden—Joyce Hague

Wine
Compliments of Paul Mann

Maytime Musicale
Grosse Pointe Park

Experience the pleasures of a spring afternoon on the shores of Lake St. Clair with lyrical music and a medley of savories and sweets.

Saturday, May 22, 1993
7:00 p.m.

Menu
Hors d'oeuvres
Smoked Salmon on Toasted Baguette with Capers,
Red Onions and Alouette Cheese
Beef and Spinach Roll with Mustard Sauce
Vermont Cheddar on Granny Smith Apple Slices
Garnished with Fresh Dill
Amish Duck Cakes with Spicy Corn Relish
Water Chestnuts wrapped in Bacon
Deep-Fried Chicken Fingers with
Sweet-and-Sour Sauce
Sweet Delights

Champagne

Hosts
Dr. and Mrs. Kim Lie

Music
St. Clair Trio:
Emmanuelle Boisvert, DSO Concertmaster, Violin
Marcy Chanteaux, Violoncello
Pauline Martin, Piano

Food
Compliments of Sparky Herberts Catering

Crisp Roast Duck with Port Wine Glaze

Port Wine Glaze

1¼	cups port
2	medium garlic cloves, slivered
4	sprigs of fresh thyme

Duck

1	(5-pound) whole duckling
	Salt and pepper to taste

For the glaze, bring the wine, garlic and thyme to a boil in a small saucepan and reduce the heat to medium-low. Simmer for 25 to 30 minutes or until the glaze is slightly thickened and reduced to 1/4 cup. Remove the garlic and thyme and discard.

For the duck, trim any fat from the duck and discard with the neck and giblets. Position the duck breast side up on a V-rack in a large roasting pan. Add enough water to the pan to come just below the bottom of the duck. Bring to a boil over high heat. Cover and reduce the heat to medium to maintain a slow steady boil. Steam for 40 minutes or until the skin has pulled away from at least 1 leg, adding additional water to maintain the water level as necessary. Place in a 400-degree oven. Roast for 35 minutes. Brush with the glaze. Roast for 10 minutes longer or until the skin is golden brown and crisp. Remove from the oven and let stand for 10 minutes before carving.

Serves 2 or 3

Poultry

Cailles Confites aux Olives et sa Garniture Forestieres
(Quail with Olives and Wild Mushroom Garnish)

Quail

8	quail
	Salt and pepper to taste
1/2	cup olives, or to taste
6	ounces smoked pork belly, chopped
8	garlic cloves, sliced
8	juniper berries
	Thyme and black peppercorns to taste
1/4	cup olive oil
1	glass of brandy
2	to 3 cups chicken stock

Garniture

2	pounds potatoes
3	to 4 tablespoons butter
	Wild mushrooms (such as morels, trumpet of death, chanterelle) to taste, chopped
1/2	cup chopped shallots
	Butter

For the quail, clean and truss the quail, discarding the head and wing tips. Season with salt and pepper. Place on a rack in a large roasting pan.

Combine the olives and pork belly in a small saucepan. Cover with water. Bring to a boil. Boil for 2 minutes. Plunge immediately into cold water and drain. Arrange over the quail. Sprinkle with garlic, juniper berries, thyme, peppercorns and olive oil. Add the brandy and chicken stock. Roast, covered, at 375 degrees for 1 to 1 1/2 hours or until the quail are tender.

For the garniture, peel the potatoes and cut into slices. Fry the potatoes in 3 to 4 tablespoons butter in a skillet until golden brown. Sauté the mushrooms and shallots in butter in a skillet until tender. Add to the potatoes and toss to mix well.

Serve the garniture with the quail.

Serves 8

Seafood

Seafood

Broiled Cajun Catfish and Black-Eyed Pea Salsa

Black-Eyed Pea Salsa

1	cup dried black-eyed peas
4	cups reduced-fat chicken stock
	Salt and pepper to taste
1	cup chopped fresh tomatoes
1/2	cup chopped red onion
2	green onions, thinly sliced
2	tablespoons chopped fresh cilantro
1/4	cup balsamic vinegar
2	tablespoons olive oil

Collard Greens

2	bunches fresh collard greens
1	smoked turkey wing
8	to 10 cups reduced-sodium chicken stock

Rice

1	cup uncooked long grain white rice
2	cups reduced-sodium chicken stock

Broiled Cajun Catfish

1	(7-ounce) catfish fillet
2	tablespoons Cajun seasoning
	Salt and pepper to taste
	Juice of 1/2 lemon

For the salsa, sort and rinse the black-eyed peas. Bring the black-eyed peas and chicken stock to a boil in a medium saucepan. Season with salt and pepper. Reduce the heat. Simmer for 1 hour or until tender; drain. Rinse the black-eyed peas; drain. Combine the black-eyed peas, tomatoes, red onion, green onions, cilantro, balsamic vinegar, olive oil and salt and pepper in a small bowl and mix well. Marinate, covered, in the refrigerator until ready to serve.

For the collard greens, remove the collard greens from the stems and tear into 2-inch pieces. Rinse 2 to 3 times; drain. Combine the collard greens, turkey and 8 cups chicken stock in a large saucepan. Bring to a boil over high heat. Boil for 40 to 60 minutes or until the collard greens are tender, adding more chicken stock as needed.

For the rice, bring the rice and 2 cups chicken stock to a boil in a saucepan. Reduce the heat. Simmer for 5 to 10 minutes or until the stock is absorbed.

For the fish, arrange the fish on a baking sheet. Season with Cajun seasoning, salt and pepper. Sprinkle with the lemon juice. Broil for 15 minutes or until the fish flakes easily.

Serve the fish with the black-eyed pea salsa, collard greens and rice.

Serves 4

Baked Flounder Creole Style

1	(3-pound) flounder, filleted
	Salt and pepper to taste
1/4	cup (1/2 stick) butter, melted
1/3	cup green bell pepper strips
1/4	cup finely chopped onion
2	tablespoons butter
1 1/2	cups chopped tomatoes
1/4	cup sliced stuffed green olives
1	teaspoon sugar
1/4	teaspoon salt
	Dash of pepper

Sprinkle the fish with salt and pepper to taste. Arrange skin side down in a buttered shallow baking dish. Pour 1/4 cup butter over the fish. Bake at 350 degrees for 25 minutes.

Sauté the bell pepper and onion in 2 tablespoons butter in a skillet until the onion is light brown. Add the tomatoes, olives, sugar, 1/4 teaspoon salt and a dash of pepper. Spoon over the fish. Bake for 10 minutes longer or until the fish flakes easily.

Serves 4

During the 1998 European tour, the musicians arrived at the hotel in Prague too late to have dinner before the concert. After the concert, Don Baker jumped on the first bus back to the hotel so he could try to have dinner at the restaurant in the hotel. Only he, Brian Ventura, assistant Principal Oboe, and Emmanuelle Boisvert, concertmaster, made it just in time. Other musicians were not so lucky; the restaurant was closed! The trio enjoyed a fabulous sautéed sole, which Don has been trying to duplicate ever since!

Seafood

Quick Halibut Steaks for Two

1   tablespoon minced parsley
1/4   teaspoon salt
1/4   teaspoon grated lemon zest or lime zest
1/8   teaspoon pepper
1   pound Alaska halibut steaks
2   tablespoons lemon or lime juice
1   tablespoon butter or margarine, melted

Mix the parsley, salt, lemon zest and pepper in a small bowl. Sprinkle the fish with the parsley mixture. Arrange in a greased shallow baking dish. Drizzle with the lemon juice and butter. Bake at 450 degrees for 10 minutes per inch of thickness or until the fish flakes easily.

Serves 2

Orange Roughy with Feta Cheese

4   (6-ounce) orange roughy fillets
1/2   cup thinly sliced onion
1   cup thinly sliced red and yellow bell peppers
1/3   cup white wine
1/2   teaspoon oregano
1/2   teaspoon salt
1/4   teaspoon pepper
1/2   cup feta cheese

Arrange the fish in a nonstick shallow baking dish. Cover with the onion and bell peppers. Pour the wine over the top. Sprinkle with the oregano, salt, pepper and feta cheese. Bake, covered, at 450 degrees for 15 to 25 minutes or until the fish flakes easily.

Serves 4

Salmon Mornay

1   (16-ounce) can water-pack salmon
2   tablespoons finely chopped onion
3   tablespoons butter
1/4   cup flour
1 1/4   cups milk
2   egg yolks, lightly beaten
2   tablespoons chopped parsley
1/4   cup grated Parmesan cheese
1/3   cup grated Swiss cheese
    Salt and pepper to taste
1   tablespoon lemon juice
1/4   cup coarse cracker crumbs
1   tablespoon butter, melted

Drain the salmon. Flake the salmon into large chunks, discarding the skin and bones. Arrange the salmon in a shallow 1-quart baking dish.

Sauté the onion in 3 tablespoons butter in a skillet for 3 minutes, being careful not to let the butter brown. Stir in the flour. Add the milk. Cook over low heat until the sauce boils and thickens, stirring constantly. Remove from the heat. Stir a few tablespoons of the sauce into the beaten egg yolks; stir the egg yolks into the hot sauce. Add the parsley, Parmesan cheese and Swiss cheese. Return to the heat. Cook until the Swiss cheese melts, stirring constantly. Season with salt and pepper. Remove from the heat. Stir in the lemon juice. Pour over the salmon.

Mix the cracker crumbs with 1 tablespoon butter in a bowl. Sprinkle over the top. Bake at 350 degrees for 20 minutes or until bubbly and light brown.

Serves 4 or 5

Portrait in Elegance
Detroit

An internationally renowned portrait artist invites you to her English country manor to tour the gallery and view her work in progress. One fortunate guest will return to have a small watercolor portrait painted.

Sunday, June 2, 1991
6:00 p.m.

Menu
Chicken Bordelaise
Seafood Mornay (at left)
Giamelli al Burro Persemane (Pasta)
Spinach Soufflé
Insalata te Caprese
French Bread with Herbed Butter
"Reine de Saba" (Queen of Sheba dessert)
Open Bar and Appropriate wines

Hosts
Robert and Patricia Burnett-Siler

Music
Catherine Compton, DSOH Viola
Marcy Chanteaux, DSOH Violoncello
Beethoven's *"Duet with two Eyeglasses Obbligato"*

Flowers
Terry's Enchanted Garden

Eastern Shore Dinner
Grosse Pointe

Michigan can't provide us with an ocean, but—
ask anyone—our lakes make a reasonable substitute,
especially when the view is accompanied by a
Jimmy Schmidt meal! A September afternoon
should provide the perfect opportunity to appreciate
the water, the boats and the freighters while the
guests delight in a seafood feast under a tent
at the water's edge.

Menu
Oysters
Crab cakes
Seared Five-Spice Salmon with
Gingered Blood Oranges (at right)
Corn on the Cob
Assorted Pastries
Coffee and Tea
Wines will be selected to complement the menu

Tuesday, September 12, 2000
6:30 p.m.

Your Hosts
Barbara and D. J. Kennedy

Catering
Jimmy Schmidt

Musical Performance
Marcy Chanteaux, Piano
Mario Di Fiore, Cello

Seared Five-Spice Salmon with Gingered Blood Oranges

4	Atlantic salmon fillets, skinned, trimmed
	Chinese five-spice powder, sea salt and freshly ground pepper to taste
	Canola oil
1	tablespoon julienned fresh ginger
	Red chile flakes to taste
1/2	cup julienned red onion
4	Belgian endives, cored, julienned
1/4	cup orange juice
	Juice of 4 Moro blood oranges
2	tablespoons honey
2	cups spinach leaves
4	Moro blood oranges, peeled, sectioned
1/4	cup cilantro leaves

Sprinkle the salmon with five-spice powder, sea salt and pepper. Sear in a hot skillet coated with oil; turn. Cook over medium heat until the salmon flakes easily. Remove to a platter; keep warm.

Sauté the ginger and chile flakes in a few drops of oil in a skillet over medium-high heat for 1 minute. Add the onion. Sauté for 2 to 3 minutes or until softened. Add the endives. Sauté for 1 minute. Add the orange juices and honey. Cook until the liquid is reduced enough to coat the vegetables. Season with salt and pepper. Add the spinach. Cook until the spinach wilts. Remove from the heat. Stir in the oranges and 1/2 of the cilantro.

To serve, mound the vegetable mixture in the center of each serving plate. Arrange the salmon on top of each. Spoon the remaining sauce over the salmon. Sprinkle with the remaining cilantro. Serve immediately.

Serves 4

Seafood

Salmon in Wine Sauce with Spaghetti Squash

Salmon

1	(3- to 4-pound) salmon fillet
2	teaspoons salt
1	teaspoon freshly ground pepper
1/4	cup lemon juice
1	large shallot, minced
2	teaspoons butter
1	cup chicken stock
1/2	cup dry white wine
1	teaspoon dill

Spaghetti Squash

2	pounds spaghetti squash
1 1/2	cups water
	Salt and pepper to taste
	Chopped fresh parsley to taste
	Tomato rose or carrot daisy

For the salmon, score the salmon into serving portions. Arrange in a shallow baking dish. Season with salt and pepper. Pour the lemon juice over the salmon. Marinate, covered, in the refrigerator for 1 hour or longer.

Sauté the shallot in the butter in a skillet until transparent. Add the chicken stock. Simmer for 5 minutes. Add the wine. Simmer for 2 to 3 minutes. Pour over the salmon. Sprinkle with the dill. Bake at 375 degrees for 15 to 20 minutes or until the salmon is firm to the touch, basting frequently with the sauce.

For the spaghetti squash, cut the squash into 1 1/2-inch rings and remove the seeds. Arrange the rings in a baking dish. Add the water. Bake, covered with foil, at 375 degrees for 15 minutes. Uncover the squash and drain the excess liquid. Bake for 5 to 10 minutes longer or until the squash is still firm to the touch. Do not overbake. Remove from the oven and cool for 15 to 20 minutes. Fork the squash within each ring to produce long strands resembling spaghetti. Season with salt and pepper. Sprinkle each with chopped fresh parsley. Arrange a tomato rose or carrot daisy on the top of each. Keep warm.

To assemble, place the salmon with sauce on a serving platter. Arrange the mounded squash rings around the salmon.

Serves 6 to 8

A conductor, who shall remain nameless, was conducting the Detroit Symphony Orchestra in a performance of a Nielson symphony at a subscription concert. He began the opening measures incorrectly and had to stop and begin again.

Two years later, as Sixten Ehrling was about to rehearse the same symphony, he stopped and said to the Orchestra, "Is this the symphony that starts twice?"

Glazed Sea Bass with Ginger Butter Sauce

Sea Bass

1/4   cup soy sauce
2   tablespoons honey
1   tablespoon rice wine vinegar
1 1/2 teaspoons cornstarch
1 1/2 tablespoons cold water
4   (6-ounce) sea bass skinless fillets

Ginger Butter Sauce

1   cup dry white wine
1/3   cup chopped shallots
1/3   cup thinly sliced fresh ginger
1/2   cup heavy cream
4   tablespoons unsalted butter, cut into 4 pieces
       Salt and white pepper to taste

For the sea bass, mix the soy sauce, honey and rice wine vinegar in a heavy saucepan. Mix the cornstarch and cold water in a small bowl. Add to the soy sauce mixture. Cook over medium heat for 2 minutes or until slightly thickened, stirring constantly. Remove from the heat to cool. Arrange the sea bass on a baking sheet. Brush with the soy sauce mixture. Bake at 350 degrees for 15 to 20 minutes or until the fish flakes easily.

For the sauce, combine the wine, shallots and ginger in a small heavy saucepan. Bring to a boil over high heat. Boil until the mixture is reduced to 1/4 cup. Add the cream. Cook until the mixture is reduced by 1/2. Remove from the heat. Strain into another saucepan, discarding the solids. Bring to a simmer. Add the butter 1 piece at a time, whisking constantly. Season with salt and white pepper to taste.

To serve, spoon the sauce onto 4 serving plates. Place the sea bass in the center.

Serves 4

Seafood

Grilled Swordfish with Sesame Sauce

Sesame Sauce

$1/2$ tablespoon sesame oil
$2^1/2$ tablespoons thinly sliced shallots
$1^1/2$ tablespoons sliced peeled gingerroot
2   teaspoons sliced garlic
$1/2$ cup rice vinegar
$1/2$ cup dry white wine
$1/2$ bay leaf
$2/3$ cup chicken stock
$1/2$ cup veal stock
$1/2$ tablespoon tahini
$1/2$ tablespoon soy sauce
$1/2$ teaspoon rice vinegar

Grilled Swordfish

2   (6-ounce) swordfish steaks
   Olive oil
   Salt and white pepper to taste
   Toasted sesame seeds
   Minced fresh parsley

For the sauce, heat the sesame oil in a skillet over medium-high heat. Add the shallots, ginger and garlic. Sauté for 1 minute. Add $1/2$ cup rice vinegar, wine and bay leaf. Bring to a boil. Cook for 25 minutes or until reduced to a glaze consistency, stirring frequently. Add the chicken stock, veal stock, tahini and soy sauce. Boil for 20 minutes or until the mixture is reduced to $1/3$ cup. Strain through a fine sieve into a heavy saucepan, discarding the solids. Stir in $1/2$ teaspoon rice vinegar and keep warm.

For the swordfish, rub the fish with olive oil. Season with salt and white pepper. Arrange on a grill rack. Grill over hot coals for 4 to 5 minutes per side or until the fish flakes easily.

To serve, place the fish on 2 serving plates. Ladle the sesame sauce over the fish. Sprinkle with toasted sesame seeds and minced parsley.

Serves 2

Seafood

Escabèche of Tuna

1/3   cup olive oil
1   tablespoon finely chopped garlic
2   cups finely chopped onions
2   cups finely chopped red bell pepper
3/4   cup finely chopped yellow bell pepper
5   sprigs of fresh thyme, finely chopped
1   bay leaf
   Salt and pepper to taste
1/4   cup red wine vinegar
2   cups finely chopped fresh tomatoes
1/4   cup capers, rinsed, drained
4   thin slices fresh lemon
1 1/4   pounds boneless skinless tuna
1/4   cup finely chopped cilantro or parsley

Heat the olive oil in a heavy skillet. Add the garlic and onions. Sauté for 2 minutes. Add the red and yellow bell peppers. Sauté for 2 minutes. Add the thyme, bay leaf, salt, pepper and vinegar. Sauté for 1 minute. Add the tomatoes and capers. Bring to a simmer. Simmer, covered, for 10 minutes. Stir in the lemon slices.

Arrange the fish on a grill rack. Grill over hot coals until the fish flakes easily. Cut into 1-inch pieces. Add the fish and cilantro to the vegetable mixture and stir to mix well. Pour into a bowl. Cool slightly. Chill, covered, for 6 hours or longer. Reheat before serving to blend the flavors.

Serves 4

Saffron Fish

1/4   teaspoon saffron
2   tablespoons warm water
1/4   cup olive oil
2   or 3 red, yellow or orange bell peppers,
     cut into 1/4-inch strips
8   garlic cloves, finely minced
2   pounds mild white fish, such as cod
   Salt and pepper to taste

Mix the saffron in the warm water in a small bowl. Let stand for 2 to 3 minutes.

Heat the olive oil in a 12-inch ovenproof skillet over medium-high heat. Add the bell peppers. Sauté for 2 to 3 minutes, reducing the heat if the bell peppers begin to brown. Add the garlic, stirring constantly to prevent burning. Add the saffron mixture. Sauté until the liquid evaporates.

Season the fish with salt and pepper. Cut into serving-size pieces. Move the vegetables to the side of the skillet. Add the fish, placing some of the vegetable mixture over the top of each piece. Bake, covered, at 350 degrees for 10 to 12 minutes or until the fish flakes easily. Remove from the oven. Let stand for 5 minutes before serving. Serve with hot cooked rice.

Serves 6 to 8

Note: This recipe may be substituted for gefilte fish during the holidays.

Crab Cakes

1 pound fresh king crab legs
1/2 medium green bell pepper, finely chopped
1/2 medium red bell pepper, finely chopped
1/2 medium red onion, finely chopped
3/4 cup seasoned bread crumbs
1/2 cup mayonnaise
1 teaspoon Dijon mustard
1 tablespoon fresh lemon juice
1 tablespoon seasoned salt
   Salt and freshly ground pepper to taste
   Seasoned bread crumbs
1/4 cup (1/2 stick) butter
1/4 cup virgin olive oil

Place the crab legs in boiling water in a large saucepan. Boil for 15 to 18 minutes; drain. Remove the crab meat from the shell. Let stand until cool.

Combine the crab meat, bell peppers, onion, 3/4 cup bread crumbs, mayonnaise, Dijon mustard, lemon juice, seasoned salt, salt and pepper in a large bowl and mix well. Add additional mayonnaise if needed for the desired consistency. Chill, covered, for 2 hours or longer.

Shape the crab mixture into crab cakes about 3 inches in diameter and 3/4 inch thick. Coat with seasoned bread crumbs.

Melt the butter in the olive oil in a large skillet. Add the crab cakes. Cook until golden brown on each side, turning once and adding additional olive oil and butter as needed.

Makes 10 to 13 crab cakes

Ring in the Holidays
Palmer Woods

Take a holiday stroll through the luxurious ambiance of an English Tudor Revival estate as you sip cocktails and nibble on delectable delicacies. Beauty abides in the Pewabic tiles, hand carved wood accents, and etched glass dining table of this Palmer Woods historical treasure.

Menu

Miniature Grilled Chicken on Country Bread with Toasted Red Pepper and Goat Cheese
Crab Cakes (at left) with Grilled Asparagus and Mesclun Greens in a Mustard Seed Vinaigrette
Hickory Smoked Turkey Breast with Wild Mushroom and Potato served with Mustard Caper Sauce
Small Assorted Rolls and Relish Tray
Penne Pasta with Mushrooms and Roasted Garlic Sauce
Farfalle Pasta tossed with Gruyère Cheese, Morel Mushrooms and Rock Shrimp
Roulade of Beef with Roasted Pepper Sauce
Teriyaki Pork Kabobs with Mango Sweet-and-Sour Sauce
Cocktails and Wines
Miniature Pastries including Assorted Tortes, Fruit Flans and Cheese Cakes
Coffee and Tea with Flavored Creams and Shaved Chocolate

Wednesday, December 8, 1999
6:00 p.m. to 9:00 p.m.

Your Hosts
Andy and Toni McLemore, Jr.

Catering
Glenn William Catering

Musical Performance
Jeffery Zook, Flute
Marian Tanau, Violin
Haden McKay, Cello

Seafood

Sea Scallops with Fresh Fennel and Cumin

4   small fennel, trimmed
3   cups chicken stock
3   tablespoons olive oil
    Salt and freshly ground white pepper to taste
1   teaspoon cumin
1   pound sea scallops, rinsed
1   tablespoon flour
2   tablespoons Spanish sherry vinegar
    Sprig of fennel

Cut the fennel bulbs into quarters. Bring the chicken stock to a boil in a saucepan over medium heat. Add the fennel. Boil for 12 minutes or until tender. Strain the stock into a bowl, reserving the fennel. Arrange the fennel on a plate. Return 2 cups of the strained stock to the saucepan, discarding the remaining stock. Cook over medium heat until the stock is reduced to 1/4 cup.

Heat 1 tablespoon of the olive oil in a nonstick skillet over medium-high heat. Add the cooked fennel. Sauté for 3 to 5 minutes or until light colored. Add salt, white pepper and 1/2 teaspoon of the cumin. Remove from the heat and keep warm.

Pat the scallops dry. Season with salt and white pepper. Sprinkle with flour and remaining 1/2 teaspoon cumin. Heat 1 tablespoon of the olive oil in a skillet over high heat. Add the scallops. Sear for 2 minutes on each side. Remove from the heat and keep warm. Add the sherry vinegar. Cook until reduced by 1/2. Add the reduced fennel stock. Whip in the remaining 1 tablespoon olive oil. Alternate the fennel and scallops in a circle on a serving platter. Spoon the sherry sauce over the top. Garnish with a sprig of fennel.

Serves 4

Scallop and Sirloin Kabobs

1/2   teaspoon garlic powder
1/2   cup vegetable oil
3   tablespoons lemon juice
1   teaspoon salt
1/4   teaspoon freshly ground pepper
2   dashes of Tabasco sauce
1/4   teaspoon dry mustard
1/4   teaspoon sugar
1/4   teaspoon thyme
2   pounds beef sirloin, cut into 1-inch cubes
2   pounds large scallops
2   limes
1/2   to 1 cup (1 to 2 sticks) butter, melted

Mix the garlic powder, oil, lemon juice, salt, pepper, Tabasco sauce, dry mustard, sugar and thyme in a bowl. Divide the marinade equally between 2 large glass bowls. Place the beef in 1 bowl and the scallops in the other bowl. Marinate, covered, in the refrigerator for 2 hours or longer.

Cut each lime into 12 slices. Drain the beef and scallops, discarding the marinade. Thread the lime slices on metal skewers, alternating with the beef and scallops and allowing 3 to 4 lime slices per skewer. Arrange on a grill rack. Grill over hot coals for 10 to 15 minutes or until brown, turning to brown evenly. Pour the butter over the kabobs before serving. Serve with rice pilaf.

Serves 6 to 8

Note: You may substitute pieces of green bell pepper, pineapple or onion for the limes. Also, you may place the kabobs on a rack in a broiler pan and broil in the oven.

Jazzy Curried Shrimp and Chicken Stir-Fry

1	*pound medium shrimp, peeled, deveined*
1	*pound boneless skinless chicken breasts, cut into 1-inch pieces*
	Juice of 1 fresh lemon
12	*garlic cloves, crushed*
4	*to 6 tablespoons vegetable oil*
4	*to 5 teaspoons hot madras curry powder, or to taste*
1	*to 1 1/2 cups sliced broccoli*
1	*to 1 1/2 cups sliced carrots*
1	*to 1 1/2 cups pea pods, trimmed*
1	*large onion, coarsely chopped*
3	*to 4 teaspoons powdered ginger*
	Soy sauce to taste
2	*(6-ounce) packages rice pilaf, or 4 cups uncooked rice*

Place the shrimp and chicken in a bowl. Add the lemon juice and toss to coat. Add 6 or 7 garlic cloves and mix well. Heat 2 1/2 tablespoons of the oil in a large skillet over medium heat. Add the shrimp, chicken, curry powder and enough water to make a sauce. Cook until the shrimp turn pink and the chicken is cooked through. Remove from heat. Cover and keep warm.

Heat the remaining 1 1/2 to 3 1/2 tablespoons oil in a large skillet over low to medium heat. Add the remaining garlic. Sauté lightly to flavor the oil. Add the broccoli, carrots, pea pods and onion. Season with ginger and soy sauce. Sauté until the vegetables are tender. Remove from the heat.

Prepare the rice pilaf using the package directions. Fluff with a fork and place in a large serving bowl. Add the shrimp and chicken mixture and the sautéed vegetables and toss to mix well.

Serves 8 to 10

It helps if you know the language. After the DSO's appearance at the Lucerne Easter Music Festival in Switzerland in 1995, Don Baker and Rob Conway traveled to Paris, Brussels, and London before coming home. They had many wonderful meals, but Rob fell on bad luck in Brussels. In Brussels, one must eat mussels; they are always wonderful. Rob, not being a fan of shellfish, however, ordered what he thought was going to be veal, never mind that he didn't know what the word was after "veal" on the menu. It turned out to be "kidneys." He had ordered very rare veal kidneys. The waiter was insulted when asked to return them to the kitchen to be cooked further. After two more trips to the kitchen he still couldn't eat them and went hungry that night.

Seafood

Saffron Cream Risotto with Shrimp

Shrimp

12   *large or jumbo shrimp*
Olive oil to taste
Minced garlic to taste
Olive oil for sautéing

Roasted Tomato Wedges

3   *to 4 medium tomatoes, cut into wedges*
Olive oil to taste
Minced garlic to taste
Salt and pepper to taste

Saffron Cream

Heavy pinch of saffron
Chopped onion to taste
3   *cups white wine*
1   *cup heavy cream*
Salt and pepper to taste

Risotto

6   *cups fresh greens, such as beet greens,*
     spinach and parsley
Olive oil for sautéing
4   *cups cooked risotto*
Salt and pepper to taste
Shaved Parmesan cheese to taste

For the shrimp, peel the shrimp, leaving the tails intact and reserving the shells for the Saffron Cream. Mix olive oil to taste and garlic in a bowl. Add the shrimp. Marinate, covered, in the refrigerator for 2 to 3 hours. Drain the shrimp, discarding the marinade. Sauté in olive oil in a skillet over high heat for 3 to 5 minutes or until the shrimp turn pink.

For the tomatoes, arrange the tomatoes in a baking pan. Sprinkle with olive oil, garlic, salt and pepper. Bake at 300 degrees for 45 minutes or until light brown.

For the Saffron Cream, combine the saffron, reserved shrimp shells, onion and wine in a saucepan. Bring to a boil and reduce the heat. Simmer, uncovered, for 45 minutes. Strain the mixture, discarding the solids. Return the mixture to the saucepan. Bring to a boil. Add the cream. Reduce the heat. Simmer until slightly thickened, stirring constantly. Season with salt and pepper. Remove from the heat and keep warm.

For the risotto, blanch the greens in boiling water in a saucepan; drain. Squeeze out as much of the water as possible. Sauté the blanched greens in olive oil in a skillet. Add the cooked risotto gradually, stirring constantly. Add the Saffron Cream gradually, stirring constantly. Cook until the mixture is creamy. Adjust the seasonings to taste.

To serve, place the Saffron Cream Risotto in the center of each serving plate. Sprinkle with Parmesan cheese. Stand 3 shrimp evenly spaced around the risotto. Arrange the roasted tomato wedges between the shrimp.

Serves 4

Shrimp Acapulco

12   (12- to 15-count) shrimp
1/4   cup (1/2 stick) butter, melted
1/4   cup olive oil
2   garlic cloves, crushed
2   dashes of Tabasco sauce
   Juice of 1 large lemon
   Juice of 1 small lime
   Salt and pepper to taste
   Paprika to taste
   Finely chopped fresh parsley to taste

Cut the fins from 1 side of each shrimp with scissors. Cut the shrimp and shell on the top side all the way back, leaving the tail intact. Butterfly each shrimp. Arrange shell side down in a shallow baking dish.

Process the butter, olive oil, garlic cloves, Tabasco sauce, lemon juice and lime juice in a blender until blended. Pour over the shrimp. Season with salt and pepper. Sprinkle with paprika. Marinate at room temperature for 15 minutes.

Bake at 400 degrees for 12 minutes or until the shrimp turn pink. Turn the shrimp over to moisten with the sauce. Sprinkle with finely chopped parsley. Serve with the sauce.

Serves 2

Johannes Brahms
German Composer
(1833–1897)

As a celebrated composer, Brahms conducted his two piano concertos in Berlin and attended a dinner given for him. His host proposed a toast to "the most famous composer." Brahms, seeing what was coming, interposed hastily, "Quite right: here's to Mozart!" and clinked glasses all round.

Seafood

Tempura of Lobster and Shrimp Mousseline in Zucchini Blossom

Mousseline in Zucchini Blossom

2   (1 1/2-pound) live lobsters, cooked
10 (16- to 20-count) shrimp, peeled, deveined
1   egg
2   tablespoons mixed basil, tarragon and parsley
1   tablespoon chopped green onions
1/2 cup sautéed sliced shiitake mushrooms
1   teaspoon ginger juice
1   teaspoon soy sauce
1   teaspoon sweet sake
    Pepper to taste
20 zucchini blossoms
1   egg
2   cups cold water
2   cups cake flour
    Vegetable oil for frying

Ginger Dashi Broth

1   (2×8-inch) konbu (dry kelp)
4   cups water
1   cup dried shaved bonito
1/3 cup soy sauce
1/2 cup sweet sake
1   teaspoon freshly grated ginger
1   teaspoon freshly grated daikon

Assembly

Oba leaves
Daikon sprouts
Togarashi (dried chiles)

For the Mousseline, Remove the lobster from the tail, claws and knuckles, discarding the shell. Chop the lobster into 1/4-inch pieces. Chop the shrimp in a bowl. Mix with a spatula until the shrimp becomes sticky and tight. Add the lobsters and mix well. Add 1 egg. Mix until the mixture is sticky. Add the mixed herbs, green onions, mushrooms, ginger juice, soy sauce and sake and mix well. Season with salt and pepper. Spoon into a pastry bag fitted with a star tip. Pipe into the zucchini blossoms, filling 2/3 full. Place on a tray.

Beat 1 egg with the cold water in a bowl. Place 2 cups of the egg water in a medium bowl. Add the cake flour a small amount at a time, mixing constantly. Do not overmix. Coat the stuffed zucchini blossoms lightly with the batter. Heat the oil to 330 degrees in a large skillet. Add the lightly coated blossoms 1 at a time, being careful not to overcrowd. Cook for 3 minutes or until golden brown. Season with salt and pepper.

For the ginger dashi broth, place the konbu in the water in a saucepan. Bring to a boil over medium heat. Discard the konbu. Remove the broth from the heat. Stir in the bonito. Let stand for 15 minutes. Strain through fine mesh into a bowl, discarding the solids. Place 2 cups of the broth in a saucepan. Add the soy sauce and sake. Bring to a boil over medium heat. Add the ginger and daikon. Remove from the heat and keep warm.

To assemble and serve, cut each zucchini blossom into halves and arrange in a serving bowl. Add 2 tablespoons of the ginger dashi broth. Sprinkle with Oba leaves, daikon sprouts and togarashi. Serve immediately.

Serves 10

128

Millie's Shrimp and Lobster

3/4	cup (1 1/2 sticks) butter	3	pounds shrimp, cooked, peeled, deveined
1/4	cup flour		
1/4	teaspoon nutmeg	6	egg yolks
	Dash of paprika	3 1/2	cups half-and-half
2	teaspoons salt	2	(6-ounce) cans lobster, drained
	Worcestershire sauce to taste		

Melt the butter in a skillet. Add the flour and stir until smooth. Add the nutmeg, paprika, salt, Worcestershire sauce and shrimp. Beat the egg yolks lightly in a bowl. Add the half-and-half and mix well. Add to the shrimp mixture. Cook for 15 minutes or until thickened, stirring constantly. Stir in the lobster. Cook until heated through. Serve with rice.

Serves 8 to 10

Wild Rice Seafood Casserole

2	(5-ounce) lobster tails, cooked, peeled	1/2	teaspoon paprika
1 1/2	pounds shrimp, cooked, peeled, deveined	1/2	teaspoon each salt, pepper and thyme
8	ounces fresh mushrooms, sliced	1	bay leaf, crumbled
		2	(10-ounce) cans cream of mushroom soup
1	cup sliced celery	1/4	cup milk
1	medium onion, chopped	1/4	cup chopped parsley
1/4	cup (1/2 stick) butter	1/2	cup slivered almonds, toasted
1	cup wild rice, cooked		

Cut the lobster and shrimp into pieces. Drain the seafood well. Sauté the mushrooms, celery and onion in the butter in a skillet for 5 minutes. Mix the rice, sautéed vegetables and drained seafood in a bowl. Add the seasonings. Stir in the soup, milk and parsley. Spoon into a lightly greased baking dish. Sprinkle with almonds. Bake, covered, at 350 degrees for 45 minutes or until heated through.

Serves 6 to 8

In Bergen, Norway, on the 1989 Detroit Symphony Orchestra tour, Don Baker and Bob Sorton, oboists, were invited for dinner at the home of the principal oboe player from the Bergen Symphony. Also present were the oboe player's family and some students. In Norway, pickled fish is a delicacy, and many people make their own at home. They use different fish and different brines. Apparently, pickled fish is an acquired taste for Americans, and Don has a pretty adventurous palate. Don said the various fishes were awful! Some were mushy and some were tough. Bob and Don politely ate what they were served but were surprised at how much they disliked it. Their host also served homemade wine and beer. The wine was unrecognizable as what we would consider wine. A wonderful host and oboe player, but, Don said, he'd never make it as a chef in the U.S.

Interludes

Pasta & Side Dishes

Pasta

P a s t a

Artichoke Pasta Strata

4   (14-ounce) cans artichokes, drained
1¹/2 pounds linguini, cooked, drained
¹/4 to ¹/2 cup (¹/2 to 1 stick) butter, sliced
2   cups grated Muenster cheese
2   cups grated Swiss cheese
1¹/2 cups grated Parmesan cheese
1   cup mayonnaise

Cut each artichoke into halves or quarters. Toss the hot pasta with the butter in a large saucepan. Divide the pasta between 2 buttered 9×13-inch glass baking dishes. Arrange the artichokes on top of the pasta to form 12 squares in each dish. Combine the Muenster cheese, Swiss cheese and Parmesan cheese in a bowl and toss with 2 forks to mix. Add the mayonnaise and toss to mix. Spread over the top of each dish.

Arrange each baking dish on the bottom oven rack. Bake at 375 degrees for 15 minutes. Remove the baking dishes to the top oven rack. Bake for 15 minutes longer or until the cheese is light golden brown. Drain any accumulated butter. Cut into squares and serve warm.

Serves 24

*Note: You may prepare this dish ahead
and store, covered, in the refrigerator
or freezer before baking.*

Fettuccini with Asparagus and Herbs

1   pound uncooked fettuccini
     Salt to taste
1   pound asparagus spears
2¹/2 tablespoons butter
1   tablespoon chopped fresh parsley
1   tablespoon chopped fresh basil
1¹/4 cups cream
     Pepper to taste
¹/2 cup freshly grated Parmesan cheese

Cook the pasta in boiling salted water in a saucepan until al dente; drain and keep warm. Trim the asparagus and cut into bite-size pieces.

Sauté the asparagus in the butter in a skillet over medium heat for 2 minutes or until tender. Add the parsley, basil and cream. Season with salt and pepper. Cook for 2 minutes, stirring constantly. Stir in the Parmesan cheese. Add to the hot pasta and toss gently to coat.

Serves 6

134

Bell Pepper Feta Pasta Toss

6	ounces uncooked linguini	1/4	teaspoon salt
1	large yellow or red bell pepper, cut into 1/8-inch strips	4	ounces crumbled feta cheese with basil and sun-dried tomatoes
1 1/4	cups quartered cherry tomatoes	1/4	cup sliced black olives
3/4	cup finely chopped fresh parsley		

Cook the pasta using the package directions, omitting the salt and vegetable oil. Place the bell pepper in a colander. Drain the pasta over the bell pepper to cook slightly. Combine the pasta, bell pepper, tomatoes, parsley, salt, feta cheese and olives in a large bowl and toss gently.

Serves 4

Broccoli with Rigatoni

1/2	cup olive oil	1	pound rigatoni, cooked, drained
2	tablespoons butter		Chopped fresh parsley to taste
4	to 6 garlic cloves, minced		Pepper to taste
1	bunch broccoli, cut into florets		Grated Romano or Parmesan cheese
1	cup chicken broth	1/2	cup coarsely chopped fresh basil
1/2	cup coarsely chopped fresh basil		

Heat the olive oil and butter in a large skillet. Add the garlic. Sauté until light brown. Add the broccoli and sauté gently. Add the chicken broth. Simmer, covered, until the broccoli is tender-crisp. Add 1/2 cup basil and hot pasta and toss to mix. Spoon into a hot serving dish. Sprinkle with parsley, pepper, Romano cheese and 1/2 cup basil.

Serves 4

Pasta

Cavatelli alla Boscaiola

1 cup dried porcini mushrooms
2 tablespoons extra-virgin olive oil
1 garlic clove, finely chopped
1 cup veal stock
1 cup heavy cream
1 to 1 1/4 pounds uncooked cavatelli
Salt to taste
1/2 cup grated Parmesan cheese

Soak the mushrooms in warm water to cover in a bowl for 30 minutes or until soft; drain and squeeze dry. Chop finely. Heat the olive oil in a large saucepan over low heat. Add the garlic. Sauté for 2 minutes or until translucent. Add the mushrooms. Sauté for 3 minutes. Add the veal stock. Cook, covered, for 5 minutes. Stir in the cream.

Cook the pasta in boiling salted water in a large saucepan until al dente; drain. Add to the sauce and toss gently over low heat. Sprinkle with the Parmesan cheese. Serve immediately.

Serves 6 to 8

Stuffed Shells Florentine

1 pound large pasta shells
1 (10-ounce) package frozen spinach, thawed
15 ounces ricotta cheese
1 cup cottage cheese
1 teaspoon basil
2 tablespoons finely chopped parsley
1 egg
Salt and pepper to taste
1/2 cup grated Parmesan cheese
Marinara sauce
2 cups mozzarella cheese

Cook the pasta using the package directions; drain. Squeeze the excess liquid from the thawed spinach. Process the ricotta cheese, cottage cheese, basil, parsley, egg, salt, pepper and Parmesan cheese in a blender until smooth. Stir in the spinach.

Pour marinara sauce into a 9×13-inch baking dish. Stuff the pasta shells with the spinach mixture. Arrange in the prepared dish. Pour marinara sauce over the pasta.

Bake, covered, at 350 degrees for 40 minutes. Uncover and sprinkle with mozzarella cheese. Bake for 10 minutes or until the mozzarella cheese melts.

Serves 8

Penne with Tomatoes and Olives

3	tablespoons olive oil
1 1/2	cups chopped onions
1	teaspoon minced garlic
3	(28-ounce) cans Italian plum tomatoes, drained
2	teaspoons dried basil
1 1/2	teaspoons crushed red pepper
2	cups canned reduced-sodium chicken broth
	Salt and black pepper to taste
1	pound uncooked penne or rigatoni
3	tablespoons olive oil
2 1/2	cups packed grated Havarti cheese
1/3	cup sliced kalamata olives
1/3	cup grated Parmesan cheese
1/4	cup finely chopped fresh basil

Heat 3 tablespoons olive oil in a large heavy Dutch oven over medium-high heat. Add the onions and garlic. Sauté for 5 minutes or until the onions are translucent. Stir in the tomatoes, dried basil and red pepper. Bring to a boil, stirring to break up the tomatoes with the back of a spoon. Add the chicken broth. Return to a boil and reduce the heat to medium. Simmer for 1 hour and 10 minutes or until the mixture is reduced to 6 cups and is of a thick chunky consistency, stirring occasionally. Season with salt and black pepper.

Cook the pasta in boiling salted water in a large stockpot until al dente. Drain the pasta and return to the stockpot. Add 3 tablespoons olive oil and toss to coat. Add the sauce and toss to mix. Add the Havarti cheese and mix well. Pour into a large nonstick baking dish. Sprinkle with the olives and Parmesan cheese. Bake at 375 degrees for 30 minutes or until heated through. Sprinkle with the fresh basil.

Serves 4

During the DSO's first European tour in 1979, following the morning rehearsal in Paris, one musician (who shall remain anonymous) asked a second musician (who shall also remain anonymous): "Are you doing anything interesting for lunch?" To which the second musician replied: "Yes, as a matter of fact. I have done a bit of research and I am going to what I am told is as fine a restaurant as there is here in Paris." Being a French speaker and lover of French cuisine, the first musician asked: "May I accompany you?" To which the second musician replied: "Well, if you want to but I am in a bit of a hurry." Following a very brisk and circuitous walk along the boulevards and streets and through the backstreets and alleys of Paris, they at last arrived at a corner at which the second musician said: "It is here, just around the corner." They turned the corner, and before them stood a McDonald's. The profanities that the first musician heaped upon the second shall remain forever hidden behind their twin shields of anonymity.

Pasta

Macaroni Salad

8   ounces uncooked elbow macaroni
     Salt to taste
     Few drops of olive oil
4   ounces hard salami, cut into tiny pieces
1   medium tomato, finely chopped, drained
1   medium green bell pepper, finely chopped
1   small bunch fresh parsley, trimmed,
        finely chopped
1/4 onion, grated, or to taste
1/2 small garlic clove, crushed
1/4 (5/8-ounce) jar Italian seasoning
     Seasoned salt and garlic-seasoned pepper to taste
     Italian salad dressing

Cook the pasta in boiling salted water in a large saucepan until al dente. Rinse with cold water; drain. Add a few drops of olive oil and toss to coat.

Combine the pasta, salami, tomato, bell pepper, parsley, onion, garlic, Italian seasoning, seasoned salt, salt and garlic-seasoned pepper in a large bowl and toss to mix well. Add enough Italian salad dressing to moisten slightly and toss to mix.

Serves 4 or 5

Mexican Manicotti

8   ounces ground beef or turkey
1   cup fat-free refried beans
1   teaspoon oregano
1/2 teaspoon cumin
8   uncooked manicotti shells
1 1/4 cups water
1   cup picante sauce
1   cup reduced-fat sour cream
1/4 cup finely chopped green onions
1/4 cup sliced black olives
1/2 cup shredded Colby-Jack cheese

Combine the ground beef, beans, oregano and cumin in a bowl and mix well. Fill the uncooked pasta shells with the ground beef mixture. Arrange in a 7×11-inch microwave-safe baking dish. Mix the water and picante sauce in a bowl. Pour over the stuffed shells. Cover with vented plastic wrap.

Microwave on High for 10 minutes, turning the dish a 1/2 turn once. Turn the pasta shells over using tongs. Microwave, covered, on Medium for 17 to 19 minutes or until the pasta is tender and the filling is cooked through, turning the dish a 1/2 turn once.

Combine the sour cream, green onions and olives in a bowl and mix well. Spoon down the center of the baking dish. Sprinkle with the Colby-Jack cheese. Microwave, uncovered, on High for 2 to 3 minutes or until the cheese melts.

Serves 4

Mom's Spaghetti and Meatballs

Meatballs

3	pounds lean ground beef	1	teaspoon basil
1	egg	1/4	teaspoon pepper
3	garlic cloves, minced		Dash of salt
2	tablespoons grated		Pinch of oregano
	Parmesan cheese		Pinch of Italian seasoning
1	tablespoon parsley		Vegetable oil for frying

Sauce

1	(28-ounce) can tomato	1	teaspoon sugar
	purée	1	teaspoon oregano
2	(6-ounce) cans tomato paste	1	teaspoon basil
2	(14-ounce) cans tomato	1/2	teaspoon Italian seasoning
	sauce	3	green bell peppers, chopped
1/4	to 1/2 cup water	1	cup sliced mushrooms
2	garlic cloves, crushed	1	onion, chopped
1	tablespoon parsley		

For the meatballs, combine the ground beef, egg, garlic, Parmesan cheese, parsley, basil, pepper, salt, oregano and Italian seasoning in a bowl and mix well. Shape into 1- to 1 1/2-inch balls. Fry in hot oil in a skillet until brown. Drain on paper towels.

For the sauce, combine the tomato purée, tomato paste, tomato sauce, water, garlic, parsley, sugar, oregano, basil and Italian seasoning in a large saucepan and mix well. Stir in the bell peppers, mushrooms and onion. Add the meatballs. Bring to a boil and reduce the heat. Simmer for 3 hours. Serve over hot cooked spaghetti.

Serves 4 to 6

West Virginia Spaghetti

8	ounces bacon, chopped	4	(6-ounce) cans Italian tomato paste
1	large onion or 2 medium onions, chopped	1	pound thin spaghetti, cooked, drained
3	pounds chuck, ground twice		
2	(4-ounce) cans sliced mushrooms		

Fry the bacon in a large skillet until crisp. Drain, reserving 1/2 cup of the pan drippings in the skillet. Add the onion to the skillet. Sauté until tender. Add the ground chuck. Cook until brown, stirring until crumbly. Add the mushrooms, tomato paste and enough water to make of the desired consistency. Simmer for 1 1/2 hours. Add the hot pasta and toss to mix.

Serves 10

Lebanese Spaghetti

1	pound lean ground lamb	1/2	bunch fresh parsley, finely chopped
1/3	cup pine nuts	1/2	cup (or more) water
1	teaspoon butter	8	ounces spaghetti, cooked, drained
2	cups plain yogurt		
2	garlic cloves, crushed		

Cook the lamb in a nonstick skillet until brown and of the desired degree of doneness. Sauté the pine nuts in the butter in a small skillet until brown, watching carefully to prevent overbrowning. Combine the yogurt and garlic in a bowl. Stir in the parsley. Add enough water to make of a pourable consistency. Combine the hot pasta, lamb and pine nuts in a large serving bowl and toss to mix. Place on serving plates. Pour the yogurt mixture over the top.

Serves 4 to 6

Pasta

Seafood Lasagna

Sauce

1	yellow onion, chopped
4	garlic cloves, minced
3	tablespoons olive oil
5	cups canned plum tomatoes
1/2	cup white wine
1	tablespoon basil
2	teaspoons fennel seeds
	Salt and pepper to taste
1	cup cream
2	tablespoons Pernod
2	pounds peeled shrimp
1	pound scallops (optional)

Crab Meat Spinach Filling

3	cups ricotta cheese
8	ounces cream cheese, softened
2	eggs
1	(10-ounce) package frozen spinach, cooked, drained
1	pound lump crab meat

Assembly

9	lasagna noodles, cooked
1	to 1 1/2 pounds mozzarella cheese, shredded

For the sauce, sauté the onion and garlic in the olive oil in a skillet for 5 minutes. Add the tomatoes, white wine, basil, fennel, salt and pepper. Simmer for 45 minutes. Add the cream, Pernod, shrimp and scallops. Simmer for 5 minutes. Remove from the heat.

For the filling, beat the ricotta cheese, cream cheese and eggs in a bowl with a wooden spoon. Add the spinach and crab meat.

To assemble, layer the sauce, lasagna noodles, crab meat spinach filling and mozzarella cheese 1/2 at a time in a 9×13-inch baking dish. Bake at 350 degrees for 50 minutes.

Serves 8 to 10

Note: This recipe freezes well.

Pasta

Rotini with Smoked Whitefish

1   pound rotini
1   tablespoon chopped garlic
1/4 cup extra-virgin olive oil
1/4 cup capers, rinsed, drained
8   ounces smoked whitefish, flaked
1/3 cup pine nuts, toasted
     Freshly ground pepper to taste

Cook the pasta in boiling water in a large saucepan using the package directions; drain.

Sauté the garlic in the olive oil in a skillet until light in color. Add the capers. Sauté for 1 minute. Remove from the heat. Add the fish, pine nuts and pepper. Add to the hot pasta in a large bowl and toss to mix.

Serves 4 to 6

Note: The sauce for this dish can be prepared in the time needed to cook the pasta.

Angel Hair Pasta Salad with Smoked Salmon

1   red bell pepper
1   green bell pepper
1   yellow bell pepper
6   cups hot cooked angel hair pasta
1/4 cup Dijon mustard
1/2 cup black olive halves
1   cup artichoke heart quarters
2   ounces fresh basil, finely chopped
2   garlic cloves, minced
1   cup bottled Caesar salad dressing
1/2 cup grated Parmesan cheese
2   (1-ounce) pieces smoked salmon
     Grated Parmesan cheese and chopped basil

Roast the bell peppers over an oven flame until evenly black all over. Remove to a bowl. Let stand, covered, for 30 minutes. Rub the bell peppers under cold running water to remove the skin. Julienne the bell peppers, discarding the seeds and membranes.

Combine the bell peppers, hot pasta, Dijon mustard, olives, artichoke hearts, 2 ounces fresh basil, garlic, salad dressing and 1/2 cup Parmesan cheese in a bowl and toss to mix. Divide among 6 serving plates. Cut the salmon into 6 pieces. Place 1 piece of the salmon on the edge of each serving plate. Garnish with grated Parmesan cheese and chopped basil.

Serves 6

Spaghetti à la Vongole
(Spaghetti in Clam Sauce)
We like to call this recipe Dorati's Clam Sauce
as it was his recipe.

1   to 2 garlic cloves, sliced
2   cups chopped parsley
5   tablespoons olive oil
4   (7-ounce) cans clams in natural juice
1   (28-ounce) can peeled tomatoes
    Salt and pepper to taste
3   pounds uncooked long Italian spaghetti
1   tablespoon salt

Sauté the garlic and parsley in the olive oil in a skillet over low heat until the garlic is light brown. Add the undrained clams and tomatoes. Season with salt and pepper to taste. Cook over low heat for 1 hour or longer.

Cook the pasta in boiling water seasoned with 1 tablespoon salt in a large saucepan for 8 minutes or until al dente; drain. Pour 1/2 of the sauce over the pasta in the saucepan. Toss over low heat until mixed. Arrange on a large serving platter. Pour the remaining sauce in the center of the pasta.

Serves 6 to 8

Get Ready...Get Set...GO!
It's the "Twist-Off" vs. "Corked-Wine" Tasting!
Detroit (Riverfront)

What's hot . . . what's not? What's in . . . what's out? What do Yuppies, Buppies, and Generation X's and Y's have in common? Maybe everything . . . maybe nothing . . . maybe something in between.
But just like people from different generations, wine, too, has its distinct flavors, regions, and vineyards. Whether you are fancy/schmatzy or laid-back and relaxed, there is a wine that suits your style and matches your mood.
Follow the crowd toward a fantastic view of the Detroit River, Belle Isle, and Ambassador Bridge, from within a backdrop of avant-garde glass collectibles and oil paintings. Bottles up!

Wednesday, October 1, 1997
5:00 p.m.–9:00 p.m.

Your Hosts
Paul Huxley and Cindy Pasky (and family pets, Missy, Sherlock, and Trumbull, too!)

Menu
Hors d'oeuvres
Corked Wine
Shrimp, Specialty Cheeses and Elegant Hors d'oeuvres
Twist-Off Wine
Peanut Butter and Jelly Sandwiches
Celery with Cheez-Whiz
(and we'll let you guess the rest!)
Desserts
Corked Wine
Cheesecake and Tortes
Twist-Off Wine
Twinkies and Hostess Cupcakes
Selection of Wines
Including Stag's Leap, Newton, Columbia Crest, Tattinger, Thunderbird, Boone's Farm, MD 20-20

Musical Performance
DSO Trio
Donald Baker, oboe; Ervin Monroe, flute; and cello, to be announced

Flowers
Compliments of EXCEL in the Renaissance Center

Springtime Serenade
Bloomfield Hills

Two chefs extraordinaire prepare a medley of springtime creations in a most gracious setting.

Wednesday, May 20, 1992
7:00 p.m.

Menu
Galantine of Pheasant
Pasta with Lobster Sauce (page 145)
Sorbet
Rack of Lamb with Spring Vegetables
Peccarino Cheese and Walnut Salad
Assortment of Desserts
Wines

Your Hosts
Monsignor Anthony Tocco
Dr. and Mrs. Robert Galacz

Music
St. Clair Trio
Emmanuelle Boisvert, DSO Violin
Marcy Chanteaux, DSO Violoncello
Pauline Martin, Piano

Flowers
Compliments of
Dr. and Mrs. Robert Galacz

Wine
Compliments of Dr. and Mrs. Frank Nesi

Saffron Pasta with Lobster Sauce

1/2   *teaspoon saffron threads*
2   *tablespoons hot water*
2   *cups all-purpose flour, or 1 1/4 cups all-purpose*
     flour and 3/4 cup semolina flour
1   *tablespoon water*
3   *extra-large eggs*

Soak the saffron in the hot water in a bowl for 15 minutes. Place the all-purpose flour in a food processor container. Add the saffron mixture. Rinse the saffron container with 1 tablespoon water and add to the food processor container. Process for 2 to 3 pulses to distribute the saffron.

Add the eggs and process to form a moist crumbly mixture that sticks together when squeezed. Remove the stiff dough to a lightly floured surface. Knead to form a smooth ball. Cover with an inverted bowl. Let rest for 30 minutes. Roll the dough into a rectangle. Cut into strips to form linguini.

(continued)

P a s t a

Saffron Pasta with Lobster Sauce

Lobster

2   *(12-ounce) large lobster tails*
2   *cups water*
1/2 *small onion*
1   *small carrot*
     Peppercorns

Lobster Sauce

2   *tablespoons butter*
1   *tablespoon olive oil*
2   *shallots, chopped*
1   *garlic clove, chopped*
1/2 *cup dry vermouth*
1/2 *cup heavy cream*

Assembly

Saffron Pasta (page 144)
Salt to taste

For the lobster, peel the lobster, reserving the shells. Cut the lobster into bite-size pieces. Crush the reserved shells. Place the shells in a saucepan with the water, onion, carrot and a few peppercorns. Cook to form a lobster stock. Strain the mixture, discarding the solids. Return the liquid to the saucepan. Cook until the stock is reduced to 1/2 cup.

For the sauce, melt the butter with the olive oil in a large skillet. Add the lobster pieces. Sauté until the lobster is opaque. Do not cook completely. Remove the lobster to a warm platter and keep warm. Add the shallots and garlic to the skillet. Sauté until softened but not brown. Add the vermouth and reduced lobster stock. Cook for 5 minutes. Add the cream. Bring to a boil. Boil until the sauce is reduced slightly. Remove from the heat.

To assemble, cook the pasta in boiling salted water in a saucepan until al dente. Drain, reserving 1 cup liquid. Return the sauce to the heat and add the lobster. Cook until heated through. Remove 1/2 of the lobster to use as a garnish. Add the remaining lobster and sauce to the pasta and toss to mix well, adding as much of the reserved 1 cup liquid as needed for the desired sauce consistency. Serve on heated plates garnished with the reserved lobster pieces.

Serves 6

Note: You may use 1 teaspoon Minor's lobster base instead of preparing your own lobster stock.

Side Dishes

Side Dishes

Tex-Mex Lentil Burgers

Lentil Burgers

1   cup dried lentils
2   cups water
1/2 cup chopped onion
1/4 cup olive oil
1/2 teaspoon salt
1/2 teaspoon black pepper
2   cups fresh bread crumbs
6   slices hot pepper cheese

Guacamole

2   ripe avocados, peeled, halved
1/2 cup chopped tomato
     Juice of 1 lime
1/4 cup chopped onion
1   tablespoon mayonnaise or plain yogurt
1/2 teaspoon cumin
     Hot pepper sauce to taste
1/4 teaspoon salt
1/4 teaspoon white pepper

Assembly

6   hamburger buns
     Mayonnaise
6   lettuce leaves
6   tomato slices
     Alfalfa sprouts

For the lentil burgers, rinse and sort the lentils. Cook the lentils in the water in a saucepan until tender; drain any excess water. Mash the lentils with a potato masher in a large bowl until thick. Purée the onion, olive oil, salt and black pepper in a food processor or blender. Add to the lentils with 1 cup of the bread crumbs and mix until thoroughly combined. Chill, covered, in the refrigerator. Shape into 6 patties. Coat the top and bottom with the remaining bread crumbs. Cook the patties in a skillet sprayed with nonstick cooking spray over medium heat until the patties are crusty on both sides, turning once. Top the patties with hot pepper cheese. Heat until the cheese melts.

For the guacamole, combine the avocados, tomato, lime juice, onion, mayonnaise, cumin, hot pepper sauce, salt and white pepper in a bowl and mash with a potato masher until slightly chunky.

To assemble, place the lentil patties on the bottom halves of the hamburger buns. Top with mayonnaise, lettuce, tomato, guacamole and alfalfa sprouts. Replace the hamburger bun tops.

Serves 6

Kielbasa Baked Beans with Apples

1	cup chopped onion	5	(14-ounce) cans barbecued baked beans
2	Granny Smith or Golden Delicious apples, peeled, chopped	1	cup golden raisins
1 1/2	to 2 pounds smoked kielbasa with garlic, sliced and scored	1	cup packed dark brown sugar
		3/4	cup ketchup
		6	tablespoons Dijon mustard
1	to 2 tablespoons water	1/4	cup barbecue sauce

Sauté the onion, apples and kielbasa in the water in a skillet over medium heat. Reduce the heat to low. Sauté for 10 minutes or until the onion is transparent. Combine the baked beans, raisins, brown sugar, ketchup, Dijon mustard and barbecue sauce in a large saucepan and mix well. Cook over low heat for 10 to 15 minutes or until heated through. Add the kielbasa mixture and mix well. Spoon into a large baking dish. Bake at 350 degrees for 45 minutes.

Serves 12

Broccoli Casserole

1	medium onion, chopped	1	(10-ounce) can cream of mushroom soup
1/2	cup (1 stick) margarine		
2	(10-ounce) packages frozen chopped broccoli, cooked, drained	1/2	cup milk
		8	ounces Cheez Whiz, or American cheese, cubed
1	cup rice, cooked		

Sauté the onion in the margarine in a skillet until transparent. Combine the sautéed onion, broccoli, rice, soup, milk and Cheez Whiz in a large bowl and mix well. Spoon into a 1 1/2-quart baking dish. Bake at 350 degrees for 30 minutes.

Serves 6

Note: This recipe freezes well.

Bob Williams, Principal Bassoonist, and wife Treva Womble, English horn player, were on the European tour in 1979 with the Orchestra when Antal Dorati was Music Director. While walking in downtown Munich, looking for a place to have dinner, they spotted a restaurant displaying luscious looking pork roasts in the window, complete with generous lumps of fat. They went in and ordered the pork, but avoided eating the layer of fat. The waitress noticed this and said in German, furrowing her brow, "Ah, but the fat is the best part!"

Ready to play "Hell's Angels," a Bassoon Quartet by Michael Daugherty.

Pictured, from left, are Paul Ganson, Marcus Schoon, Bob Williams, and Vicki King.

S i d e   D i s h e s

Brussels Sprouts in Mustard

2¹/2 *pounds fresh brussels sprouts*
      Salt to taste
¹/4   *cup (¹/2 stick) butter*
2   *tablespoons white mustard seeds*
¹/4   *cup coarse grain French mustard*
1   *teaspoon salt*
      Freshly ground pepper

Trim the brussels sprouts. Make a crosscut at the base of each brussels sprout. Cook in boiling salted water in a saucepan for 10 to 12 minutes or until tender-crisp; drain. Melt the butter in a large heavy skillet over medium heat. Stir in the mustard seeds and mustard. Cook until the butter is light brown, stirring constantly. Add the brussels sprouts and mix well. Season with 1 teaspoon salt and pepper. Serve immediately.

Serves 8

Braised Belgian Endives
The perfect accompaniment to pork, beef, halibut, or salmon. Divine when served with mashed potatoes (no lumps, please).

4 *Belgian endives*
3 *tablespoons butter*

Rinse the endives and pat dry. Remove the core and any brown part from the bottom. Cut each endive into halves lengthwise. Heat the butter in a large nonstick skillet over medium heat until the butter begins to bubble. Add the endives in a single layer. Cook until the endives are light brown on each side. Add just enough water to cover the bottom of the skillet. Reduce the heat to medium-low. Cook until the endives are soft and caramel brown, turning occasionally and adding additional water as needed.

Serves 4

Note: Choose Belgian endives with yellow edges only. There should be no green edges. Select the smallest ones possible. Do not use any salt or pepper, or any condiment or spice, as the endives are perfect by themselves.

Cabbage Strudel

1	(2- to 2½-pound) head cabbage, coarsely grated
2	to 3 teaspoons salt, or to taste
¼	cup vegetable oil
	Freshly ground pepper to taste
1	(17-ounce) package puff pastry, thawed
1	egg yolk
1	tablespoon cream

Place the cabbage in a bowl and sprinkle with the salt. Let stand at room temperature for 2 to 3 hours, or chill for 8 to 12 hours; drain and squeeze the cabbage to remove the excess moisture. Sauté in the oil in a large skillet until soft and brown. Season with pepper. Remove from the heat to cool.

Roll the pastry into a thin rectangle on a lightly floured surface. Spread the cabbage mixture over ½ of the pastry. Roll loosely toward the unfilled edge and seal to enclose the filling. Cut vents in the top. Arrange on a baking sheet. Brush with a mixure of the egg yolk and cream. Bake at 375 degrees for 20 to 25 minutes or until puffed and brown.

To serve, cut diagonally into slices. Serve with roast beef or game.

Serves 6 to 8

Note: You may use one 16-ounce package of phyllo pastry instead of the puff pastry. Stack 4 or 5 layers of phyllo pastry on a lightly floured board, brushing 3 to 4 tablespoons melted butter between each layer. Spread with the cabbage and roll up loosely. Arrange on a baking sheet. Brush with the egg yolk and cream. Bake at 350 degrees for 20 to 25 minutes or until brown.

Magyar Magic
Bloomfield Hills

Be transported to Budapest as two multi-talented Hungarian chefs join forces to create a Hungarian rhapsody.

Sunday, November 6, 1994
6:30 p.m.

Menu

Előételek—Appetizers
Pogácsa—Savory Biscuits
Káposztás Rétes—Cabbage Strudel (at left)
Hortobágyi Palacsinta—Chicken Paprikash in Crepes

Ebéd—Entrée
Vadas Hús—Hunter-Style Beef Roast
Kolbászal Toltott Sertés Borda—Pork Loin
Stuffed with Kolbasz
Gomboc—Dumplings
Öszi Zöldseg—Fall Vegetables

Édességek—Desserts
Dobos Torta
Apro Sütemények—Pastries

Hungarian Wines and Liqueurs

Hosts
Robert and Patricia Galacz
Beatriz Budinszky Staples

Music
Bogos Mortchikian, Violin
Joseph Striplin, Violin
Beatriz Budinszky, Viola
Minka Christoff, Violoncello
Douglas Cornelson, Clarinet

S i d e   D i s h e s

Baked Hominy with Cheese

1/4   cup (1/2 stick) butter
1/4   cup flour
2   cups light cream
2   teaspoons horseradish
      Salt and white pepper to taste
2   (15-ounce) cans white hominy, drained
1/3   cup freshly grated Parmesan cheese

Melt the butter in a medium saucepan. Whisk in the flour. Cook for 1 minute, whisking constantly. Stir in the cream, horseradish, salt and white pepper. Add the hominy and mix well. Spoon into a buttered 2-quart baking dish. Sprinkle with the Parmesan cheese. Bake, covered, at 300 degrees for 1 hour and 20 minutes.

Serves 4 to 6

Sweet-and-Sour Red Cabbage

3   quarts shredded red cabbage
1 1/2 cups finely chopped onion
1   cup water
3   tablespoons sugar
1 1/2 teaspoons salt
3   tablespoons red currant jelly
1 1/2 tablespoons vinegar

Mix the cabbage and onion in a bowl. Heat the water, sugar, salt and jelly in a saucepan until the sugar dissolves, stirring frequently. Add the cabbage mixture. Simmer, covered, for 20 minutes. Cook, uncovered, until the liquid evaporates, stirring constantly. Remove from the heat. Add the vinegar and toss well.

Serves 6 to 8

Danish Caramelized Potatoes

24   small new potatoes
1/2   cup sugar
1/2   cup (1 stick) unsalted butter, melted

Scrub the potatoes. Place in boiling water in a saucepan. Cook for 15 to 20 minutes or until tender; drain. Let stand until cool enough to handle. Peel the potatoes.

Melt the sugar in a 10- to 12-inch skillet over low heat, stirring constantly using a wooden spoon. Cook for 3 to 5 minutes or until caramelized, stirring constantly. Watch carefully to prevent burning. Stir in the melted butter. Add as many of the potatoes as possible without crowding the skillet, shaking the skillet constantly to roll the potatoes to coat. Remove to a warm bowl. Repeat the process until all of the potatoes are coated.

Serves 8

152

Pfälzer Schales

The Pfalz is a region of Germany, located on the Rhineland Palatinate and is world renowned for its beautiful forests and its outstanding white wines, especially the rieslings. Its people love to eat and drink well and plentifully.

Schales is a very simple dish and is the Pfälzer version of the Jewish schalet or scholet, which translates from the French into "warm long." It was prepared on Friday and was kept warm to be served on the Sabbath, the day any kind of work was forbidden. The Pfälzer only replaced the kosher meat with smoked bacon.

3	to 4 pounds potatoes, peeled, coarsely grated
3	or 4 large leeks, thinly sliced
2	eggs, lightly beaten
8	ounces thickly sliced smoked bacon, cubed
	Salt and freshly ground pepper to taste
	Freshly grated nutmeg to taste

Combine the potatoes, leeks, eggs, bacon, salt, pepper and nutmeg in a large bowl and mix well. Spoon into a generously greased cast-iron Dutch oven. Bake at 375 degrees for 1¹/2 hours. Serve with a green salad in a vinaigrette or sliced cucumbers in sour cream dressing. A regional riesling cabernet will complement the meal.

Serves 6 to 8

Side Dishes

Pegache

Dough

1/4 cup (105- to 115-degree) water
1 envelope dry yeast
1 teaspoon sugar
1/2 cup milk
2 1/2 to 3 cups flour
2 tablespoons sugar
1/2 teaspoon salt
1 egg, lightly beaten
2 tablespoons butter, melted
2 tablespoons vegetable oil

Filling

3 medium potatoes, peeled, chopped
Salt to taste
1 cup shredded Cheddar cheese
2 tablespoons butter
1/4 teaspoon salt

For the dough, combine the water, yeast and 1 teaspoon sugar in a bowl and stir until the sugar dissolves. Heat the milk in a saucepan to 120 to 130 degrees. Mix 1 1/2 cups of the flour, 2 tablespoons sugar and 1/2 teaspoon salt in a bowl. Make a well in the center. Stir in the egg. Add the hot milk and stir to mix well. Stir in the butter and oil. Add the yeast mixture and stir to mix well. Stir in as much of the remaining flour as possible. Turn onto a lightly floured surface. Add enough of the remaining flour to make a moderately stiff dough. Knead for 6 to 8 minutes or until smooth and elastic. Let rise, covered, until doubled in bulk.

For the filling, boil the potatoes in salted water to cover in a saucepan for 20 to 25 minutes or until tender; drain. Add the cheese, 2 tablespoons butter and 1/4 teaspoon salt. Mash until the potatoes are smooth.

To assemble, punch the dough down. Divide into 2 equal portions. Cover and let rise for 10 minutes. Roll 1 portion of the dough into a 10×15-inch rectangle. Arrange on a lightly greased baking sheet. Spread the filling to within 1 inch of the edge. Roll the remaining dough into a 10×15-inch rectangle. Place over the filling, pinching the edges to seal. Prick the top with a fork every 2 inches so the steam can escape. Bake at 400 degrees for 20 minutes. Cut into serving pieces. Serve warm or cool.

Serves 15

Note: You may wrap the individual serving pieces and store in the freezer.

Potato Kugel (Pudding)

4   medium potatoes, peeled, quartered
1/2   teaspoon seasoned salt, or to taste
1/2   teaspoon salt, or to taste
1   egg
1   large Spanish onion, sliced
     Vegetable oil

Boil the potatoes in enough water to cover in a saucepan until tender; drain. Add the seasoned salt and salt and mash well. Beat the egg in a bowl. Add 4 or 5 tablespoons of the slightly cooled potatoes and mix well. Add to the remaining potatoes and mix well. Fry the onion in oil in a skillet until brown. Spread 1/2 of the potato mixture in a 2-quart baking dish. Layer the fried onions over the potatoes, pressing into the potato mixture. Spread the remaining potatoes over the top. Bake at 350 degrees for 45 to 60 minutes or until golden brown.

Serves 4

Note: You may substitute chopped liver for the fried onion layer. To increase or decrease the number of servings, allow 1 potato per person, 1 onion for every 3 or 4 people and 1 egg per every 5 potatoes.

Sinful Potato Casserole

8   large baking potatoes, baked, cooled
1   cup chopped onion
1/2   cup (1 stick) butter
1   pound sour cream
2   cups shredded Cheddar cheese

Peel the baked potatoes. Cut into cubes into a large bowl. Sauté the onion in the butter in a skillet until golden brown. Add to the potatoes and mix well. Add the butter, sour cream and Cheddar cheese and mix well. Spoon into a 9×13-inch baking dish. Bake at 375 degrees for 30 to 40 minutes or until hot and bubbly.

Serves 8 to 12

Igor Stravinsky
(1882–1971)
Russian-born composer

Stravinsky, greatly concerned with his health, would sometimes put himself on a diet of raw vegetables. During one such period, he dined on raw tomatoes and potatoes at a restaurant with composer Nicholas Nabokov. Nabokov left some of his cutlet at the side of his place, and Stravinsky asked if he might finish it. Swallowing the morsel with a generous helping of sour cream, he declared, "I want to astonish the raw potato in my stomach."

Side Dishes

Epinards de la Mornay, Gratines

2   *(10-ounce) packages frozen spinach*
1½ *cups milk*
2   *tablespoons butter*
3   *tablespoons flour*
½   *teaspoon salt*
    Pinch of pepper
    Pinch of nutmeg
7   *tablespoons grated Swiss cheese*

Thaw the spinach in a saucepan. Heat over high heat for 2 to 3 minutes or until all excess liquid is evaporated, stirring constantly.

Heat the milk to the boiling point in a saucepan. Melt the butter in a saucepan over low heat. Blend in the flour. Cook for 2 minutes, stirring constantly. Remove from the heat. Pour in the hot milk and beat immediately with a wire whisk to mix well. Return to the heat. Bring to a boil. Cook for 1 minute, stirring constantly. Remove from the heat. Add the salt, pepper and nutmeg and mix well. Add 4 tablespoons of the cheese and stir until the cheese melts.

Add ⅔ of the sauce to the spinach and mix well. Spoon into a lightly buttered 8-inch baking dish. Spread the remaining sauce over the top. Sprinkle with the remaining 3 tablespoons cheese. Bake at 350 degrees for 30 minutes or until light brown.

Serves 8

Note: You may prepare this recipe ahead.

Spinach Pie

2   *(10-ounce) packages fresh spinach, rinsed*
3   *eggs, beaten*
2   *pounds small curd cottage cheese*
8   *ounces cream cheese, softened*
8   *ounces feta cheese, or to taste*
12 *phyllo pastry sheets (8 ounces)*
    Butter

Tear the spinach into a large bowl. Add the eggs, cottage cheese, cream cheese and feta cheese and mix well. Stack 6 pastry sheets in a buttered 9×13-inch baking pan, brushing each layer with melted butter. Spread with the cheese mixture. Stack the remaining phyllo sheets over the spinach mixture layer, brushing each layer with melted butter. Brush the top sheet generously with melted butter. Bake at 350 degrees for 45 to 60 minutes or until light brown. Remove from the oven and cool for 10 minutes. Cut into squares. Serve hot or cold.

Serves 8 to 10

Fried Green Tomatoes

2	cups cornmeal
1/4	teaspoon cayenne pepper
	Salt and black pepper to taste
4	medium green tomatoes
1	cup flour
2	cups buttermilk
1	cup corn oil

Combine the cornmeal, cayenne pepper, salt and black pepper in a bowl and mix well. Cut the green tomatoes into slices 1/4 inch thick. Season with salt and black pepper. Dust the green tomatoes with the flour. Dip in the buttermilk and then in the cornmeal mixture. Fry in the hot oil in a large cast-iron skillet over medium to high heat for 3 minutes per side. Remove to paper towels to drain.

Serves 6 to 8

Brunch with An
African American Accent
Detroit Riverfront

Enjoy the magic of the river through the windows of this perch, high above the city. After reflecting on the wonders of the view, appreciate a chance to contemplate the human triumphs of noted artists Lawrence, Bearden, and Woodruff among others. Spectacular will be the only word to adequately describe your brunch experience.

Menu
Assorted Breakfast Meats
Scrambled Eggs
Grits
Hash Brown Potatoes
Fried Apples
Fried Green Tomatoes (at left)
Jambalaya
Assorted Breads
Peach Cobbler
Bread Pudding
Pecan Sweet Potato Pie
Champagne, Mimosas and Bloody Marys
Juices, Coffee and Tea

Sunday, May 14, 2000
11:00 a.m.

Your Hosts
Arthur and Chacona Johnson

Catering
Catering Concepts Services

Musical Performance
Rick Robinson, Bass

Side Dishes

Ratatouille en Croûte

2   medium onions, coarsely chopped
2   or 3 garlic cloves, minced
2   green bell peppers, cut into 1-inch pieces
1/4 cup olive oil
1   large zucchini, cut into 1/2-inch pieces
1   large yellow squash, cut into 1/2-inch pieces
10   large mushrooms, sliced
1   large eggplant, peeled, cut into 1-inch pieces
3   tomatoes, peeled, seeded, coarsely chopped
2   teaspoons basil, crushed
1   teaspoon dry Italian salad dressing mix
1/2 teaspoon white pepper
     Salt to taste
16   phyllo sheets
1   cup (2 sticks) butter, melted
1/2 cup fine dry bread crumbs
1/2 cup grated Parmesan cheese
1 1/2 cups shredded Monterey Jack or Cassari cheese

Sauté the onions, garlic and bell peppers in the olive oil in a large saucepan for 5 to 7 minutes or until the onions are translucent. Add the zucchini, yellow squash and mushrooms. Sauté for 10 minutes. Add the eggplant. Sauté for 7 minutes. Add the tomatoes. Cook until heated through. Season with the basil, Italian salad dressing mix, white pepper and salt. Remove from the heat.

Lay the phyllo sheets on a work surface and cover with a damp towel. Lay 1 phyllo sheet in a 9×13-inch baking dish and brush generously with the melted butter. Sprinkle with 1 tablespoon of the bread crumbs and 1 tablespoon of the Parmesan cheese. Repeat the layers 7 times. Spread the vegetable mixture over the layers. Sprinkle with some of the Monterey Jack cheese. Layer 1 sheet of phyllo over the cheese. Brush generously with melted butter. Sprinkle with some of the Monterey Jack cheese. Repeat the layers with the remaining phyllo sheets, brushing each layer with melted butter and sprinkling with the Monterey Jack cheese. Tuck in the sides to enclose the filling. Brush the top with the remaining melted butter. Bake at 350 degrees for 55 to 65 minutes or until the top is brown and puffed. Let stand for 10 minutes before cutting.

Serves 6 to 8

Wild Mushroom Risotto

1	tablespoon dried wild mushrooms	1/4	cup (1/2 stick) butter
1	cup water	1	cup freshly grated Parmigiano-Reggiano
1	cup white wine	4	garlic cloves, chopped
1	onion, chopped Olive oil for sautéing	2	or 3 large portobello mushrooms, cut into 1/4-inch crescents
2	cups arborio rice		
4	cups warm chicken stock	1/4	cup chopped parsley
1	pizzicato saffron in stock		Salt and pepper to taste

Soak the wild mushrooms in the water in a bowl for 1 hour or longer. Strain the wild mushrooms, squeezing out the excess moisture and reserving the broth. Chop the wild mushrooms in a food processor.

Open the wine and taste it. If you like it, you can cook with it. The entire cooking process will take approximately 1 movement or 20 minutes. Sauté the onion in 3 half notes of olive oil in a large saucepan over medium-high heat until translucent. Add the chopped wild mushrooms. Sauté during a scherzo and a trio. Add the rice. Cook until heated through and the rice is coated, stirring constantly. Add 1/2 cup of the wine. Cook until the wine is absorbed, stirring constantly. Add the reserved dried mushroom broth, stirring until almost absorbed. Add the chicken stock 1 cup at a time, cooking after each addition until the stock is almost absorbed and the rice is cooked through and adding water if you run out of stock. Remove from the heat. Stir in the saffron in stock. Add 2 tablespoons of the butter and 1/2 cup of the cheese. Cover and let stand.

Sauté the garlic in olive oil and remaining 2 tablespoons butter. Add the portobello mushrooms. Cook for 5 minutes. Add the remaining 1/2 cup wine. Cook until most of the liquid is evaporated.

To serve, spoon the risotto onto serving plates. Top with the mushrooms, remaining 1/2 cup cheese and parsley. Season with salt and pepper. Serve with good bread, good wine and good salads.

Serves 6

Emmanuelle Boisvert

Detroit Symphony Orchestra Concertmaster Emmanuelle Boisvert was the first woman to be named concertmaster of a major American orchestra when she was appointed to the position in 1988. Only twenty-five at the time, she also made history by being one of the youngest concertmasters in the world. The *Detroit Free Press* has commented that "Boisvert's musicianship takes a back seat to no one," while the *Detroit News* has said that her playing is distinguished by "a compelling blend of technical finesse and expressive sensibility."

Emmanuelle's impressive accomplishments do not go unrecognized by Orchestra Hall patrons or by her fellow musicians. Unfortunately, her three children are not quite as dazzled by their mom's musical achievements. On a recent Mother's Day at school, one of her children was asked what Mommy does for a living. She answered, "Daddy does all the cooking. Mommy doesn't do anything!"

Side Dishes

Mushroom Crumble

Evelyn Glennie, OBE, percussionist, sends this recipe all the way from Scotland.

3   ounces wholemeal bread crumbs
6   ounces mixed nuts, ground
1   garlic clove, crushed
1   teaspoon mixed herbs or chopped fresh parsley
1/2   cup vegetable oil
1   large onion, chopped
1   tablespoon vegetable oil
8   ounces mushrooms, sliced
1/4   cup flour
1/2   cup stock
    Salt and pepper to taste

Mix the bread crumbs, mixed nuts, garlic and herbs together. Add to 1/2 cup oil in a bowl and mix well. Let stand for 1 hour. Sauté the onion in 1 tablespoon oil in a skillet until soft and brown. Add the mushrooms. Sauté until tender. Sprinkle with the flour. Cook for 2 minutes. Remove from the heat. Add the stock, stirring constantly. Return to the heat. Cook until thickened, stirring constantly. Season with salt and pepper. Pour into an ovenproof 7×11-inch baking dish. Sprinkle with the crumb mixture. Bake at 425 degrees for 30 minutes.

Serves 6 to 8

Vegetable Soufflé

1   (15-ounce) can baby carrots, drained
1   tablespoon butter
1   tablespoon brown sugar
2   (10-ounce) packages Stouffer's spinach soufflé, thawed
2   (10-ounce) packages Stouffer's corn soufflé, thawed

Sauté the carrots in the butter and brown sugar in a skillet. Layer the spinach soufflé, corn soufflé and sautéed carrots in a square 2-quart glass baking dish. Bake at 350 degrees for 1 1/2 hours or until a knife inserted in the center comes out clean.

Serves 4

Lemon Rice Pilaf

1 1/2   cups minced onions
5   tablespoons olive oil
3   cups long grain white rice
3   (14-ounce) cans chicken broth
1/2   cup fresh lemon juice
1 1/2   tablespoons grated lemon zest
3/4   teaspoon ground pepper
    Salt to taste

Sauté the onions in the olive oil in a large heavy saucepan over medium heat for 10 minutes or until tender. Add the rice. Sauté for 2 minutes. Add the broth, lemon juice, lemon zest and pepper. Bring to a boil, stirring occasionally. Reduce the heat to low. Cook, covered, for 20 minutes or until the rice is tender and the liquid is absorbed. Remove from the heat. Let stand, covered, for 5 minutes. Season with salt.

Serves 6

Bulgur Pilav

1   *large onion, finely chopped*
2   *tablespoons vegetable oil*
2   *cups bulgur (wheat), rinsed*
4   *cups chicken broth*
      Salt and pepper to taste

Sauté the onion in the oil in a skillet until the onion is almost brown. Add the bulgur and mix until the bulgur absorbs the oil. Add the broth and mix well. Bring to a boil and reduce the heat to low. Cook, covered, for 15 to 20 minutes or until the liquid is absorbed. Season with salt and pepper.

Serves 4

Note: Store, covered, in the refrigerator for
24 hours to enhance the flavor.

A Summer Place
Harbor Springs

Breathe in the beauty of Northern Michigan! Say good-bye to summer in a beautiful contemporary home overlooking Lake Michigan. The harmony of nature, incomparable music and the warm hospitality of your hosts create a perfect ending to summer.

Sunday, September 3, 1995
2:00 p.m.

Menu
Appetizers
Basterma—Dried Seasoned Beef
Lehmejoon—Pita with Meat and Vegetables
Sarma—Stuffed Grape Leaves
Cheese Beoregs
Entrée
Lamb Shish Kebobs
Bulgur Pilav (Wheat) (at left)
Ratatouille
Red Pepper Strips
Dessert
Paklava
Armenian String Cheese

Red and White Wines

Hosts
Michael and Emma Minasian

Music
Emmanuelle Boisvert, Concertmaster, DSO
Debra Fayroian, Cello
Randall Hawes, Bass Trombone
Wesley Jacobs, Tuba

Side Dishes

Tomato Pudding

1   (10-ounce) can tomato purée
1/2 cup boiling water
1   cup packed brown sugar
1/4 teaspoon salt
1 1/2 cups fresh bread cubes
1   teaspoon curry powder, or to taste
1/4 cup (1/2 stick) butter, melted

Bring the tomato purée, boiling water, brown sugar and salt to a boil in a saucepan. Cook for 5 minutes. Arrange the bread cubes in a baking dish. Sprinkle with the curry powder. Pour the melted butter over the bread cubes. Pour the hot tomato mixture over the top. Bake at 325 to 400 degrees for 30 minutes.

Serves 4

Roasted Red Pepper Compote

3/4 cup drained chopped peeled roasted red
     bell peppers
2   tablespoons olive oil
1   green onion, minced
1   garlic clove, minced
1   tablespoon fresh parsley
1 1/2 teaspoons balsamic or red wine vinegar
1 1/2 teaspoons small capers
1/8 teaspoon crushed red pepper

Combine the bell peppers, olive oil, green onion, garlic, parsley, balsamic vinegar, capers and red pepper in a bowl and mix well. Chill, covered, in the refrigerator for 2 to 3 hours. Serve with pork chops or grilled fish.

Makes 1 cup

Devonshire Country Relish

3   cups canned whole kernel corn
1 1/2 cups mincemeat
1/2 cup chopped apple
1   cup chopped sweet pickles
1/2 cup sweet pickle juice

Drain the corn. Combine the corn, mincemeat, apple, pickles and pickle juice in a saucepan and mix well. Simmer over medium heat for 15 minutes. Chill in the refrigerator. Serve on a relish tray.

Makes 6 cups

Cilantro Pesto

2¹/2 cups coarsely chopped cilantro
¹/2 cup grated Parmesan cheese
¹/2 cup pine nuts or almonds, skinned, blanched
¹/4 cup chopped garlic
¹/4 cup lime juice
1 tablespoon plus 1 teaspoon chili powder
1 tablespoon cumin
1 tablespoon crushed red pepper
1¹/2 teaspoons salt
3/4 cup olive oil
     Salt and black pepper to taste

Process the cilantro, Parmesan cheese, pine nuts, garlic, lime juice, chili powder, cumin and red pepper in a food processor until finely chopped, pulsing and scraping the side occasionally. Stir in 1¹/2 teaspoons salt. Add the olive oil in a fine stream, processing constantly until emulsified. Season with salt and black pepper to taste.

Spoon into an airtight container. Store in the refrigerator for up to 1 week or store in the freezer for up to 1 month. Serve as a sauce to grilled chicken, swordfish or salmon. Also good served on quesadillas.

Makes 3 cups

Note: Make a nice sauce for chilled shrimp by adding heavy cream in a ratio of 1 part heavy cream to 2 parts pesto.

Monsignor's Masterpiece
Bloomfield Hills

Heavenly music and divine food. Buon Appetito!

Sunday, May 22, 1994
5:00 p.m.

Menu
First Course
Melon and Prosciutto
Second Course
Fusilli with Pesto (at left)
Entrée
Galantine of Chicken with Champagne Sauce
New Potatoes
Spring Vegetables
Dessert Buffet

Appropriate Wines

Hosts
Monsignor Anthony Tocco

Music
Marguerite Deslippe, Violin
Linda Snedden-Smith, Violin
Mario DiFiore, Violoncello
Stephen Molina, Bass

Food and Wine
Underwritten by The Beef Carver, Inc.

Flowers
Compliments of Thrifty Florists.

Desserts

The French Connection
Detroit

Your Heritage House presents a display of music
for children of the French-speaking world as a setting
for an evening of French cuisine and music.

Sunday, September 17, 1995
4:00 p.m.

Menu

Hors d'oeuvre Assortis
Assorted Appetizers

Salade à la Francaise
Mixed Green Salad with Vinaigrette Dressing

Poulet á la Sauce Champagne
Chicken with Champagne Sauce

Carrottes Vichy
Glazed Parsleyed Carrots

Haricots Verts
Green Beans

Pain Baguette
French Bread

Desserts Parisien
Parisian Sweet Table

Appropriate Wines

Hosts
Bill and Johnnie Hunter
Josephine Love

Music
Marcy Chanteaux, Harpsichord
Mario DiFiore, Violoncello

Marie Antoinette Cake

Meringue

1 1/2	cups shelled hazelnuts, toasted
1/2	cup sugar
2	tablespoons cornstarch
11	extra-large egg whites
1	cup sugar

Cheesecake

20	ounces cream cheese, softened
3/4	cup sugar
1	teaspoon vanilla extract
4	extra-large eggs, at room temperature

Frosting

24	ounces cream cheese, softened
1	cup (2 sticks) unsalted butter, softened
2	teaspoons vanilla extract
8	ounces bittersweet chocolate, melted, cooled

Assembly

1	to 2 1/2 pints fresh red raspberries

Desserts

For the meringue, line 2 metal 10×11-inch baking sheets with parchment paper. Draw one 10-inch circle on each sheet with a pencil. Grease the parchment paper and lightly sprinkle with flour. Process the hazelnuts, 1/2 cup sugar and cornstarch in a food processor fitted with a steel blade until ground. Beat the egg whites in a deep medium mixing bowl until soft peaks form. Add half of the 1 cup sugar gradually, beating constantly until stiff peaks form. Fold in the remaining 1/2 cup sugar and nut mixture. Spoon into a pastry bag fitted with a plain tip. Pipe onto the circles on the prepared baking sheets in a circular motion until each circle is completely covered. Pipe the remaining mixture in 4-inch strips onto the unused portion of the parchment paper. Bake at 275 degrees for 1 1/2 to 2 hours or until dry.

For the cheesecake, line the bottom of a 10-inch springform pan with parchment paper. Grease the parchment paper and the side of the pan. Beat the cream cheese and sugar in a mixing bowl until light and fluffy. Add the vanilla and mix well. Add the eggs 1 at a time, beating well after each addition. Spoon into the prepared pan and spread to distribute evenly. Bake at 350 degrees for 30 to 35 minutes or until a wooden pick inserted in the center comes out clean. Remove from the oven to cool. Chill, covered, for 1 to 12 hours.

For the frosting, beat the cream cheese and butter in a mixing bowl until smooth and creamy. Stir in the vanilla. Add the melted chocolate and beat well until smooth.

To assemble, trim the meringue circles if needed. Place 1 meringue circle on a cardboard circle. Spread a thin layer of the frosting over the top. Pack 1/3 of the raspberries on the frosting. Cover with additional frosting. Release the side of the springform pan. Remove the chilled cheesecake from the pan carefully. Place on top of the berries and frosting. Place the remaining meringue circle on top of the cheesecake. Spread with a thin layer of the frosting. Pack 1/2 of the remaining raspberries over the frosting. Cover with additional frosting. Spread the remaining frosting over the top and side of the cake. Decorate the side of the cake with the meringue strips. Arrange the remaining raspberries in the pattern of your choice over the top of the cake.

Serves 12

D e s s e r t s

Black Russian Cake

Cake

1	(2-layer) package moist yellow cake mix without pudding
1	(6-ounce) package chocolate instant pudding mix
4	eggs
1/2	cup sugar
1	cup vegetable oil
1/4	cup vodka
1/4	cup coffee-flavor liqueur
3/4	cup water

Glaze

1/4	cup coffee-flavor liqueur
1	cup confectioners' sugar

For the cake, combine the cake mix, pudding mix, eggs, sugar, oil, vodka, liqueur and water in a large mixing bowl. Beat for 4 minutes. Pour into a well-greased bundt pan. Bake at 350 degrees for 40 minutes or until a wooden pick inserted in the center comes out clean. Cool on a wire rack.

For the glaze, combine the liqueur and 1/2 cup of the confectioners' sugar in a small mixing bowl and beat until smooth.

To assemble, invert the cake onto a cake plate. Poke holes in the top of the cake several times using the tines of a fork. Cover with the glaze. Sprinkle with the remaning 1/2 cup confectioners' sugar.

Serves 12

Cocoa Cake

This World War I cake recipe contains no eggs.

1	teaspoon baking soda
1	cup sour milk
13/4	cups flour
1/4	cup baking cocoa
1/2	cup (1 stick) butter, softened
1	cup sugar

Stir the baking soda into the sour milk. Mix the flour and baking cocoa together. Beat the butter and sugar in a mixing bowl until light and fluffy. Add the sour milk mixture and flour mixture alternately, beating well after each addition. Pour into a greased 8-inch square cake pan. Bake at 350 degrees for 20 to 30 minutes or until the cake tests done.

Serves 4 to 6

Note: To make sour milk, use 1 tablespoon vinegar or lemon juice for every cup of milk. Let stand at room temperature for 10 minutes or until curdled. Buttermilk may also be used instead of sour milk.

Molten Lava Cakes

8   ounces bittersweet chocolate, finely chopped
1   cup (2 sticks) unsalted butter
6   eggs
1¹/2 cups sugar
¹/2 cup flour

Butter the bottom and sides of fifteen 4-ounce ramekins. Sprinkle with sugar, tapping to remove the excess sugar. Melt the chocolate and butter in a double boiler over simmering water, whisking constantly. Beat the eggs, 1¹/2 cups sugar and flour in a mixing bowl with a whisk until blended. Add the chocolate mixture gradually, whisking constantly. Pour ¹/3 cup of the mixture into each prepared ramekin. Arrange the ramekins on a baking sheet. Bake at 400 degrees for 10 to 12 minutes or until the tops are firm and beginning to crack and the edges are set. Remove from the oven. Serve immediately with your favorite ice cream.

Serves 15

Note: The exterior of the cakes should be cakelike while the center should remain soft and runny.

Lakeside Winds
Bloomfield Hills

Supper on the veranda overlooking Kirk in the Hills and Island Lake. Mrs. Robinson will show you her artistic works and her special glass collection.

A week-end evening in July, 1990

Menu
Smoked Fish Salad
Cheese Puffs
Chicken Breast with Italian Sauce
Basmati Rice with Wild Pecans
Marinated Vegetable Salad
White Peach Mousse
Chocolate Decadence

Hosts
Mr. and Mrs. Jack Robinson

Music
Doug Cornelson and DSOH Wind Ensemble

Flowers and Wine
Compliments of the host

Lemon Meringue Sponge Cake

Lemon Sponge Cake

8	egg yolks		Grated zest of 1/2 lemon
1 1/2	cups sugar	1	cup sifted matzo cake meal
1/8	teaspoon salt	8	egg whites
	Juice of 1/2 lemon		

Lemon Topping

3	eggs	Juice of 3 lemons
1 1/2	cups sugar	

Creamy Meringue Icing

2	egg whites	1/2	cup water
1	cup sugar	1	cup grated walnuts

For the cake, beat the egg yolks in a mixing bowl until light. Add the sugar and beat well. Add the salt, lemon juice, lemon zest and cake meal and mix well. Beat the egg whites in a mixing bowl until stiff peaks form. Fold into the batter. Pour into an ungreased 3-quart glass baking dish. Bake at 350 degrees for 45 minutes or until the cake pops back when lightly touched. Remove from the oven to cool on a wire rack.

For the topping, beat the eggs in a saucepan. Add the sugar and beat well. Add the lemon juice gradually, beating constantly at low speed. Cook over low heat until thickened, stirring constantly with a wooden spoon. Remove from the heat. Let stand until cool.

For the icing, beat the egg whites in a mixing bowl until stiff peaks form. Cook the sugar and water in a saucepan over low heat to 270 to 290 degrees on a candy thermometer, soft-crack stage. Remove from the heat. Pour gradually over the edge of the bowl into the stiffly beaten egg whites, beating constantly until the mixture is creamy and thick.

To assemble, spread the topping over the cake. Spread the icing over the top. Sprinkle with the walnuts.

Serves 6 to 8

D e s s e r t s

Drunken Prune Cake

Prunes

20   *pitted prunes, cut into quarters*
1/2   *cup madeira, ruby port or orange juice*

Cake Batter

3   *large eggs*
1   *cup sugar*
3/4   *cup (1 1/2 sticks) unsalted butter, softened*
1 1/2   *cups unbleached flour*
2   *teaspoons baking powder*
1/3   *cup freshly squeezed orange juice*
1   *teaspoon vanilla extract*
1/4   *teaspoon nutmeg*
1/2   *teaspoon (scant) salt*

Custard

1/3   *cup sugar*
1   *tablespoon plus 1 teaspoon cornstarch*
3/4   *cup scalded milk*
2   *egg yolks*
      Grated zest of 1 orange
1   *teaspoon vanilla extract*

Assembly

Confectioners' sugar

For the prunes, combine the prunes and wine in a small bowl. Let stand, covered, at room temperature for 8 to 12 hours or until plump.

For the batter, process the eggs, sugar and butter in a food processor for 15 seconds, stopping once to scrape the bowl. Add the flour, baking powder, orange juice, vanilla, nutmeg and salt. Process for 5 seconds or until smooth, stopping once to scrape the bowl.

For the custard, mix the sugar and cornstarch in a small saucepan. Add the milk in a fine stream, stirring constantly. Whisk in the egg yolks. Cook over low heat for 8 to 10 minutes or until thickened, stirring constantly. Do not boil. Remove from the heat. Stir in the orange zest and vanilla. Set in a larger pan of cold water. Beat for 1 minute to cool the custard.

For the assembly, spread a scant 1/2 of the cake batter evenly in a thin layer in a greased and floured nonstick 9-inch springform pan. Drop the custard by spoonfuls over the batter and spread evenly with a knife, leaving a 1/2-inch margin around the outside edge. Dot the custard layer with the prunes. Drizzle any remaining wine over the top. Drop the remaining batter by spoonfuls over the prunes and spread evenly with a knife to cover the prunes. Level the top. Bake at 400 degrees on the middle oven rack for 35 to 45 minutes. Reduce the oven temperature to 350 degrees. Bake for 15 minutes longer or until the cake pulls from the side of the pan and the center is risen and brown. Remove the pan to a wire rack to cool completely. Loosen the cake from the edge of the pan with a knife. Release the edge of the pan. Arrange on a dessert plate. Sprinkle with confectioners' sugar. Keep covered with plastic wrap until ready to serve. Serve plain or with a dollop of whipped cream.

Serves 8

Just Desserts
West Bloomfield

A fabulous dessert buffet with complementary wines and informal commentary by Larry Shade of Gibbs World Wide Wines will make this a truly sweet summer evening.

Sunday, June 9, 1991
7:00 p.m.

Menu
All Prepared by your Hostess!
Apricot Pistachio Torte with Honey Butter Cream
Chocolate Velvet Four Seasons Cake
Strawberry Charlotte
Nectarine Mousse Cake
Fruit Tart
Peanut Butter Chiffon Cake
Peppermint Chocolate Loaf
Coconut Cake with Lemon Filling
Pear Kuchin
Raspberry Cheesecake
Grasshopper Pie
Pineapple Trifle
Tropical Storm Cake
Wine Cream Roll
Assorted Cookies

Hosts
Susan S. Thoms, M.D. and
David M. Thoms, Esq.

Music
Paul Wingert, DSOH Violoncello
Joseph Striplin, DSOH Violin
Beatriz Budinszky, DSOH Violin

Wine
Gibbs World Wide Wines

Flowers
Rosenman's Flowers

Trio of Chocolate Mousses

Dark Chocolate Mousse

2	egg yolks
1/2	tablespoon sugar
1	tablespoon mocha paste
3	ounces dark chocolate, melted
1/4	cup whipping cream, whipped
2	egg whites
2	tablespoons sugar

Milk Chocolate Mousse

1	tablespoon unflavored gelatin
2	tablespoons cold water
1	egg
1	egg yolk
4	ounces milk chocolate, melted
2	tablespoons dark rum (optional)
3/4	cup whipping cream, whipped

White Chocolate Mousse

1	teaspoon unflavored gelatin
2	tablespoons cold water
1	egg
1	egg yolk
4	ounces white chocolate, melted
2	tablespoons cherry liqueur (optional)
3/4	cup whipping cream, whipped

Raspberry Coulis

1	(10-ounce) package frozen raspberries
	Sugar to taste
	Sprigs of fresh mint

Desserts

For the Dark Chocolate Mousse, beat the egg yolks and 1/2 tablespoon sugar in a medium mixing bowl until light and pale yellow. Beat in the mocha paste and dark chocolate. Fold in the whipped cream. Beat the egg whites and 2 tablespoons sugar in a mixing bowl until stiff peaks form. Fold into the chocolate mixture. Pour into a 2-inch deep dish. Chill, covered with plastic wrap, for 8 hours or longer.

For the Milk Chocolate Mousse, sprinkle the gelatin in the cold water in a saucepan. Let stand for 10 minutes or until softened. Heat over low heat until the gelatin is dissolved, stirring constantly. Beat the egg and egg yolk in a medium mixing bowl until thick and pale yellow. Add the milk chocolate and rum gradually, stirring constantly. Stir in the gelatin mixture. Fold in the whipped cream. Pour into a 2-inch deep dish. Chill, covered with plastic wrap, for 8 hours or longer.

For the White Chocolate Mousse, sprinkle the gelatin in the cold water in a saucepan. Let stand for 10 minutes or until softened. Heat over low heat until the gelatin is dissolved, stirring constantly. Beat the egg and egg yolk in a medium mixing bowl until thick and pale yellow. Add the white chocolate and cherry liqueur gradually, stirring constantly. Stir in the gelatin mixture. Fold in the whipped cream. Pour into a 2-inch deep dish. Chill, covered with plastic wrap, for 8 hours or longer.

For the Raspberry Coulis, strain the raspberries, reserving the juice. Place the raspberries, reserved juice and sugar to taste in a medium saucepan. Heat until the sugar dissolves, stirring constantly. Chill in the refrigerator.

To serve, place a pool of Raspberry Coulis on each chilled serving plate. Dip a serving spoon or ice cream scoop into hot water. Place a scoop of each mousse on the sauce. Garnish with fresh mint.

Serves 8

Note: You may substitute 2 cups of anglaise sauce for the raspberry coulis if desired.

When Jean-Pierre Rampal visited the home of Ervin Monroe, Principal flutist, Monroe's wife, Susan, offered their guest Cointreau straight up. He insisted she return it to the kitchen and serve it to everyone over cracked ice, which, he explained, to be the ideal serving for this liqueur, his favorite. The Cointreau turned from clear to a milky color when poured over the cracked ice, and Susan pointed this out to the renowned flutist. "Ah, yes," he said, "and it tastes as good as mother's milk, too!"

This crepe recipe is a delicious post-concert snack that is easy to prepare and offers limitless variations on a theme. "Curtain-Call" Crepes taste best when accompanied by Jean-Pierre Rampal's recording of the *Jazz Suite* by Claude Bolling for flute, piano, bass, and drums, or Ervin Monroe and Patti Masri-Fletcher's flute and harp recording entitled *After a Dream*.

"Curtain Call" Crepes

Crepes

1	cup flour	1 1/2	cups milk
1/2	teaspoon salt	4	eggs
1	teaspoon sugar		

Filling

1	pound small curd cottage cheese	1	teaspoon grated orange zest
2	eggs		Raisins to taste
1/4	cup sugar		Cointreau or your favorite liqueur or grape juice
1	teaspoon grated lemon zest		

Assembly

1/2	cup (1 stick) butter		Sour cream

For the crepes, combine the flour, salt, sugar, milk and eggs in a bowl and mix well. Pour 1/2 cup of the batter into a buttered skillet, rocking the skillet so the batter spreads evenly over the bottom. Cook until brown on 1 side. Place cooked side down on a paper towel. Repeat with the remaining batter, continuing to stack the crepes. Store, wrapped, in the refrigerator for up to 2 days.

For the filling, combine the cottage cheese, eggs, sugar, lemon zest and orange zest in a mixing bowl and beat well. Soak the raisins in enough Cointreau to cover in a bowl for 24 hours.

To assemble, place a heaping tablespoonful of the filling in the middle of the brown side of each crepe. Add some of the raisins if desired. Tuck in the ends and fold over the sides. Melt the butter in a skillet. Add the crepes. Cook until light brown on both sides. Serve with a small amount of sour cream and the raisins.

Serves 12

Desserts

Pear and Apple Crostata

Pastry

1	cup all-purpose flour
2	tablespoons whole wheat flour
2	tablespoons sugar
1/4	teaspoon salt
1/4	cup (1/2 stick) unsalted butter
1/4	cup shortening, chilled
2	tablespoons (or more) ice water

Filling

2	Granny Smith apples, peeled, quartered, sliced
1	Anjou pear, peeled, quartered, thinly sliced
3	tablespoons brown sugar
2 1/2	tablespoons minced crystallized ginger
1	tablespoon flour
2	teaspoons fresh lemon juice

Assembly

1	large egg, beaten
1	tablespoon sugar

Topping (optional)

1/2	cup whipping cream
1 1/2	teaspoons honey
1/4	teaspoon Chinese five-spice powder

For the pastry, process the all-purpose flour, whole wheat flour, sugar and salt in a food processor. Add the butter and shortening and process until crumbly. Add enough ice water to form moist clumps, processing constantly. Wrap in plastic wrap. Chill for 1 hour or until firm.

For the filling, combine the apples, pear, brown sugar, ginger, flour and lemon juice in a bowl and toss to mix well. Let stand until the juices form.

To assemble, roll the pastry into a 12-inch circle on a floured surface. Mound the filling on the top, leaving a 2-inch border. Fold the border over the filling. Brush with the beaten egg. Sprinkle with 1 tablespoon sugar. Arrange on a baking sheet. Bake at 400 degrees for 40 minutes.

For the topping, beat the whipping cream, honey and five-spice powder in a bowl until soft peaks form.

To serve, cut the crostata into wedges and arrange on serving plates. Top with a dollop of the topping.

Serves 6 to 8

Desserts

Pumpkin and Caramel Cheesecake

Crust

2   cups graham cracker crumbs
1/4 cup sugar
1   tablespoon cinnamon
1/4 cup (1/2 stick) butter, melted

Caramel

3   cups sugar
2   cups cold water
     Juice of 1 lemon
2   cups heavy cream

Filling

48   ounces cream cheese, softened
1/4 cup flour
2   cups pumpkin purée
1   tablespoon vanilla extract
2   tablespoons nutmeg
7   eggs

Assembly

1   cup warm bittersweet chocolate sauce
     Confectioners' sugar
     Sprigs of fresh mint

For the crust, line a 4-inch-deep 12-inch round cake pan with parchment paper. Mix the graham cracker crumbs, sugar, cinnamon and butter in a bowl. Press over the bottom of the prepared pan.

For the caramel, bring the sugar, water and lemon juice to a simmer in a medium nonreactive skillet over high heat. Cook to 310 degrees on a candy thermometer, hard-crack stage. Remove from the heat. Add the heavy cream in a fine stream, whisking constantly until combined. Return to the heat. Cook for 10 minutes or until thickened. Remove from the heat. Let stand until warm.

For the filling, beat the cream cheese in a large mixing bowl until smooth. Add 2 cups of the warm caramel and flour and blend until smooth, scraping down the side of the bowl. Add the pumpkin, vanilla and nutmeg and mix well. Beat in the eggs 1 at a time, scraping down the side of the bowl.

To assemble, pour the filling into the prepared pan. Place in a larger pan. Add enough water to come 2/3 of the way up the cake pan. Place on the lower oven rack. Bake at 300 degrees for 1 1/4 to 1 1/2 hours or until the center is set. Remove from the water bath to a wire rack. Pour the remaining caramel over the top. Cool to room temperature. Chill, covered, for 8 to 12 hours.

To serve, unmold the cheesecake from the pan. Cut into 12 slices. Place on individual dessert plates. Drizzle the chocolate sauce artistically over the cheesecake slices and the plates. Sprinkle with confectioners' sugar. Garnish with fresh mint.

Serves 12

Sopaipillas

These hollow "soft pillows" of bread are immediate favorites of all those who try them. They are easy to make if the shortening is very hot and only a few are fried at a time. History reveals they originated in Old Town, Albuquerque, about three hundred years ago.

1   envelope dry yeast
1/4   cup warm (105 to 115 degrees) water
1¹/2   cups (about) scalded milk, cooled
4   cups sifted flour
1¹/2   teaspoons salt, or to taste
1   teaspoon baking powder
1   tablespoon shortening or butter
4   cups shortening or vegetable oil

Dissolve the yeast in the warm water in a bowl. Add to the cooled scalded milk in a bowl. Mix the flour, salt and baking powder in a bowl. Cut in 1 tablespoon shortening until crumbly. Make a well in the center. Add about 1¹/4 cups of the yeast mixture and mix to form a soft dough. Add the remaining yeast mixture, mixing to form a firm dough that holds its shape. Place on a lightly floured surface. Knead 15 to 20 times or until smooth. Invert the bowl over the dough. Let rest for 10 minutes. Divide the dough into 4 equal portions. Roll each portion into a rectangle or circle ¹/4 inch thick. Cut into squares or triangles. Do not reroll the dough. Cover with a towel.

Heat 4 cups shortening to 400 degrees in a deep fryer. Fry the dough squares a few at a time in the hot shortening, pushing under until puffed and hollow; keep the remaining dough squares covered. Drain on paper towels. Serve with honey.

Makes 4 dozen

Viva Argentina!
Bloomfield Hills

Classical guitar evokes the sophisticated culture and cuisine of Argentina in a lake-front home designed by award winning architect Carl Lukenbach.

Sunday, May 19th
12:30 p.m.

Menu
Aperitivos
Arrolados de Palmitos con Jamon
Tarta de Berenjena
Entrada
Empanadas de Carne, de Espinaca,
y de Cebolla y Jamon
Brochettes de Pollo
Tarteletas de Humita
Postres
Alfajores
Panuelos de Dulce de Leche
Tartas de Fruta
Trufas

Appropriate Wines

Hosts
Mr. and Mrs. Byron Trerice, Jr.

Music
Gale Benson, guitar

Flowers
Compliments of the host

Mad About Chopin
Dearborn
Garden sculpture and a collection of crystal and artwork set the stage for this classic Polish dinner.

Saturday, May 14, 1994
6:00 p.m.

Menu

Zakaski—Appetizers
First Course
Vodka Toast
Zupa Poziómkova—Strawberry Soup
Salata Wiosna—Spring Salad
Entrée
Cielecina z Sos Grzybowy—
Veal with Imported Polish Mushrooms
i Wiosne Jarzyny—Spring Vegetables
Dessert
Nalésniki—Crepes
Mazurek
Polish Torte (at right)
The torte is a family recipe, which was published by Neiman Marcus in their cookbook, *Pigtails and Frogslegs.*

Appropriate Wines

Hosts

Stanley and Gloria Nycek
Richard and Mary Dee Dryer

Music

Leszek Bartkiewiez, Piano

Wine

Compliments of Mr. and Mrs. Mark Anusbigian,
Westborn International Market

Flowers

Compliments of Mr. Bruce Weber,
Weber's Floral Gifts.

Polish Torte

Cake

1	cup ground nuts
1	cup dry rye bread crumbs
1	teaspoon baking powder
10	egg yolks
1	cup confectioners' sugar
1/2	teaspoon almond extract
10	egg whites, stiffly beaten

Coffee Frosting

5	eggs
1	cup sugar
1	teaspoon instant coffee
2	teaspoons water
1	cup plus 2 tablespoons butter
2	teaspoons Kahlúa
	A few drops of water

For the cake, butter a 9-inch springform pan. Sprinkle with bread crumbs. Mix the nuts, 1 cup bread crumbs and baking powder together. Beat the egg yolks, confectioners' sugar and flavoring in a mixing bowl until smooth. Stir in the nut mixture. Fold in the egg whites. Pour into the prepared pan. Bake at 400 degrees for 15 minutes. Reduce the oven temperature to 350 degrees. Bake for 30 minutes. Cool on a wire rack.

For the frosting, beat the eggs and sugar in a double boiler. Cook over hot water until thickened, stirring constantly. Remove from the heat to cool, stirring occasionally. Dissolve the coffee in 2 teaspoons water in a bowl. Cream the butter in a mixing bowl. Beat in the egg and coffee mixtures. Cut the cake horizontally into 3 layers. Brush each layer with a mixture of the Kahlúa and a few drops of water. Spread the frosting between the layers. Chill, covered, in the refrigerator.

Serves 12

Desserts

Apple Pudding

2   tablespoons flour
1¼ teaspoons baking powder
⅛   teaspoon salt
1   egg
½   cup each sugar and chopped cooking apples
    Raisins, dried cherries or dried cranberries to taste
½   cup chopped nuts
1   teaspoon vanilla extract

Mix the flour, baking powder and salt together. Beat the egg and sugar in a mixing bowl until blended. Stir in the flour mixture. Add the apples, raisins, nuts and vanilla and mix well. Spoon into a buttered round baking dish. Bake at 350 degrees for 35 minutes. Serve with ice cream or whipped topping.

Serves 2 or 3

Almond Macaroons

8   ounces almond paste, cut up
1   cup sugar
2   egg whites

Process the almond paste, sugar and egg whites in a food processor until smooth. Drop by tablespoonfuls onto cookie sheets lined with brown paper. Bake at 325 degrees for 20 to 30 minutes or until golden brown. Remove to wire racks to cool. Wet the back of the brown paper to remove the macaroons.

Makes about 1 dozen

Poppy Seed Cookies

4   cups flour
1   teaspoon salt
4   teaspoons baking powder
1   cup poppy seeds
3   eggs
1½ cups sugar
3/4 cup vegetable oil
2   teaspoons vanilla extract

Sift the flour, salt and baking powder into a bowl. Stir in the poppy seeds. Beat the eggs and sugar in a mixing bowl. Add the oil and vanilla and beat well. Add the flour mixture and mix well. Roll the dough into a thin rectangle on a well-floured surface using a floured rolling pin. Cut into desired shapes using a floured cookie cutter. Arrange on ungreased cookie sheets. Bake at 375 degrees for 12 to 15 minutes or until golden brown.

Makes 4 dozen

Note: The older the cookies get (if they last that long), the crisper and more delicious they become.

Desserts

Double-Lemon Bars

1½ cups flour
¼ cup confectioners' sugar
¾ cup (1½ sticks) unsalted butter
6 eggs
3 cups sugar
Zest of 2 lemons
1 cup plus 2 tablespoons fresh lemon juice
½ cup flour
Confectioners' sugar

Process 1½ cups flour, ¼ cup confectioners' sugar and cold butter in a food processor until crumbly. Press over the bottom and ¾ inch up the side of a 9×13-inch baking pan. Bake at 350 degrees for 20 to 30 minutes or until golden brown. Remove from the oven and cool slightly.

Beat the eggs, sugar, lemon zest and lemon juice in a mixing bowl with a whisk. Sift ½ cup flour over the egg mixture. Blend until smooth. Pour into the baked crust. Bake at 300 degrees for 35 minutes or until set. Remove to a wire rack to cool completely. Cut into bars. Sprinkle with confectioners' sugar.

Makes 2 dozen

Old German Recipe Sour Cream Cookies

4½ to 5 cups flour
½ teaspoon salt
1 teaspoon baking soda
4 teaspoons baking powder
Nutmeg to taste
2 cups sugar
1 cup shortening
2 eggs, beaten
1 teaspoon vanilla extract
1 cup sour cream
1 cup chopped toasted walnuts (optional)
1 cup raisins (optional)

Mix 4½ cups of the flour, salt, baking soda, baking powder and nutmeg together. Beat the sugar and shortening in a mixing bowl until light and fluffy. Add the eggs and beat well. Beat in the vanilla. Add the sour cream and flour mixture alternately, beating well after each addition and adding ½ cup flour if needed for the desired consistency. Stir in the walnuts and raisins. Drop by tablespoonfuls onto greased cookie sheets. Bake at 350 degrees for 15 to 18 minutes or until the cookies are brown around the edge. Cool on the cookie sheets for a few minutes. Remove to a wire rack to cool completely.

Makes 4 dozen

Salzburger Nockerl
(Austrian Soufflé)

2	egg yolks
1/4	cup Grand Marnier
1/2	teaspoon vanilla extract
1/4	teaspoon almond extract
1/4	teaspoon orange extract
1/4	cup sugar
3/4	cup flour
16	egg whites (2 cups)
	Pinch of cream of tartar
3/4	cup sugar
2	tablespoons cream
	Confectioners' sugar

Combine the egg yolks, Grand Marnier, vanilla, almond extract, orange extract and 1/4 cup sugar in a medium-large stainless steel bowl and mix well. Add the flour and mix well.

Beat the egg whites and cream of tartar in a stainless steel bowl until the mixture begins to thicken. Add 3/4 cup sugar gradually, beating constantly until stiff peaks form. Add 1 cup of the beaten egg whites to the flour mixture and mix until smooth. Fold in the remaining beaten egg whites.

Spread the cream on an ovenproof plate. Heap the mixture onto the prepared plate. Bake at 400 degrees for 10 minutes. Reduce the oven temperature to 325 degrees. Bake for 10 to 15 minutes longer or until golden brown. Remove from the oven. Sprinkle with confectioners' sugar and serve immediately.

Serves 6 to 8

Meet the Maestro
Grosse Pointe

DSO Music Director Neeme Järvi and his wife, Liilia, request the pleasure of your company for an evening of music, conversation, and hospitality at the home of DSO Executive Director Mark Volpe and his wife, Martha.

Sunday, September 26, 1993
6:30 p.m.

Menu
Hors d'oeuvres
Siberian Pelmeni
Herbed Caviar Roulade
Finnish Canapés
Swedish Herring Salad
Beet Caviar with Walnuts and Prunes
Chicken Liver Pâté
Marinated Mushrooms
Variety of Smoked Fish
Gravlax
Accompanied by Horseradish and Assorted Mustards
White, Rye and Pumpernickel Breads
Flavored Vodkas
Sweet Table

Hosts
Maestro Neeme and Liilia Järvi
Mark and Martha Volpe

Music
Ervin Monroe, DSO Flute
Patricia Masri-Fletcher, DSO Harp

Desserts

Blueberry Sour Cream Pie

1/2 cup plus 3 tablespoons light brown sugar
2   cups fresh blueberries
2   tablespoons flour
2   cups sour cream
1   egg
1   (10-inch) graham cracker pie shell

Toss 1/2 cup brown sugar and blueberries in a bowl. Beat the flour, 3 tablespoons brown sugar, sour cream and egg in a bowl. Layer 1/2 of the sour cream mixture, the blueberry mixture and remaining sour cream mixture in the pie shell. Bake at 400 degrees for 10 minutes or until set. Cool slightly. Cover and chill.

Serves 8

Key Lime Pie

4   eggs, separated
1   (14-ounce) can sweetened condensed milk
1/2 cup Key lime juice
1   (10-inch) graham cracker pie shell
6   tablespoons sugar
1/2 teaspoon cream of tartar

Beat the yolks in a bowl until pale yellow. Beat in the condensed milk and lime juice. Pour into the pie shell. Beat the whites in a bowl until soft peaks form. Beat in the sugar and cream of tartar gradually until stiff. Spread over the pie. Bake at 350 degrees until brown.

Serves 8

Sweet Potato Pie

2   large sweet potatoes
1   egg
1/4 cup (1/2 stick) unsalted butter
6   ounces sweetened condensed milk
1/4 teaspoon lemon juice
1/2 teaspoon vanilla extract
1/2 teaspoon nutmeg
1/2 teaspoon cinnamon
     Pinch of salt
     Sugar to taste
     Brown sugar to taste
1   partially baked (10-inch) pie shell

Boil the unpeeled sweet potatoes in enough water to cover in a saucepan until tender; drain. Let stand until cool enough to handle. Peel the sweet potatoes. Combine the sweet potatoes, egg, butter, condensed milk, lemon juice, vanilla, nutmeg, cinnamon, salt, sugar and brown sugar in a mixing bowl and beat until smooth. Pour into the partially baked pie shell. Bake at 350 degrees for 20 minutes or until firm.

Serves 8

Apple Streusel Tarts

1	cup plus 2 tablespoons sugar	1	tablespoon cinnamon
2	cups (4 sticks) butter	1	cup sugar
4	eggs	1	cup flour
	Pinch of salt	1	teaspoon salt
1	teaspoon almond extract	1 1/2	teaspoons baking powder
5 1/4	cups flour	1/2	cup (1 stick) butter, cubed
6	Granny Smith apples, peeled, cored, thinly sliced	1	egg
		1	cup plus 2 tablespoons packed brown sugar
1	cup sugar	1	cup heavy cream
			Ice cream

Cream 1 cup plus 2 tablespoons sugar and 2 cups butter in a mixing bowl. Add 4 eggs, pinch of salt and almond extract and beat well. Add 5 1/4 cups flour and beat using the dough hook attachment to form a ball. Chill, covered, for 30 minutes.

Divide the dough into 12 equal portions. Roll each portion into a circle on a lightly floured surface. Line twelve 4-inch tart pans with false bottoms with the circles.

Toss the apples, 1 cup sugar and cinnamon in a bowl. Arrange in the prepared tart pans.

Pulse 1 cup sugar, 1 cup flour, 1 teaspoon salt and baking powder in a food processor. Add 1/2 cup butter and process for 1 minute. Add 1 egg and process until mixed. Spoon over the apple mixture. Bake at 325 degrees for 45 minutes. Cool slightly.

Bring 1 cup plus 2 tablespoons brown sugar and cream to a boil in a heavy saucepan. Cook until the mixture is reduced to a sauce consistency, stirring constantly.

Remove the tarts from the pans and arrange on dessert plates. Top with ice cream and the caramel sauce.

Makes 12 tarts

Contributors

The Volunteer Council would like to thank all of the individuals who contributed to this recipe collection. The enthusiastic participation of good cooks, amateur and professional, in sharing their favorite recipes is greatly appreciated. We regret that we were unable to include all of the recipes submitted due to space limitation.

Throughout Musical Feasts, *look for* *denoting a musician contributed the recipe.*

Claire Abrams
Tom Allen
Virginia Andreae
Nancy Arnold
Jean Azar
Connie Bageris
Donald Baker
Sally Baker
Marlynn Barnes
Mary Beattie
Loretta Biskup
Martha Bjorkman
Emmanuelle
   Boisvert
Marlene Boll
Bess Bonnier
Elaine Borruso
Jeanne Boucher
Carol Bozadzis
Betty Bright
Doreen Bull
Jean Carman
Lorraine Cheney
Gloria Clark
Robert Coldwell
Douglas Cornelson
Minka Cornelson
Genie Cravens
Lilit Danielyan
Michael Daugherty
Maureen D'Avanzo
Edward Deeb

Marguerite
   Deslippe-Dene
Lynne Girard
   Dewey
Mario DiFiore
Barbara Diles
Lester Doulis
Pierre Duelz
Jac Duquette
Melanie Everson
Millie Everson
Phyllis Fane
Beverly Farley
Christa Anne
   Flueck
Pamela Frank
Ruth Frank
Robert Galacz
Chris Garavaglia
Joy Garber
Teresa Giffels-Bryne
Susan Giffin
Evelyn Glennie,
   OBE
Marianne
   Glesmann
Barbara Goodwin
Paulette Groen
John Guinn
Patti Haarz
Eileen Harned
Gwen Harrington

Florence Harris
Judy Harris
Mary Hendrien
Nancy Henk
Douglas Horn
Sybil Jacques
Sandi Jarackas
Neeme Järvi
Bonnie Jobe
Debra
   JohnsonClark
Constance Johnston
Emil Kang
Paul Keller
Jeanette
   Keramedjian
Sandie Knollenberg
Gus Kokas
Helen Kokas
Maria Kokas
William Kokas
Virginia Kwyer
Vicki Lange
Barbara Lawler
Kirk Lawson
Cindy Leonard
Rita Levy
Susan Libertiny
Ruth MacRae
Barbara Madigan
Molly Markley
Nadine Matthew

Marilyn McDonald
Eva Meharry
Matt Michaels
Emma Minasian
Ervin Monroe
Patricia Nickol
Shahida Nurullab
Gloria Nycek
Kevin O'Neill
Sally Orley
Marie-Paule Parcells
Christopher
   Parkening
Eleanor Pekkala
Itzhak Perlman
Karl Pituch
Joan Reed
Heather Reickert
Alice Reisig
Fay Ann Resnick
Felix Resnick
Joseph Resnick
Andrea Rogers
Laura Rowe
Marjorie Saulson
Tillie Saunders
Winston Sawyer
Juanita Scharnweber
Marilyn Schneider
Trudi Schreiber
Patricia Senecoff
Anne Simons

Bruce Smith
Marion Smith
Julie Stackpoole
Marilyn Stanitzke
Beatriz Staples
Paula Stiefvater
Robert Stiles
Phyllis Strome
Carol Struch
Eloise Tholen
Marilyn Vadino
Barbara Vandewater
James Van
   Valkenberg
Julie Viar
Gillian von Dreble
Ursula Walker
Joseph Walsh
Melanie Resnick
   Wells
Judy Werner
Marcia Wiltshire
Ava Wixted
Olive Chung Wong
Patricia Young
Aynne Zazas
Mary Zazas
Francine Zick
Jeffery Zook

Contributors

Many of the area's finest chefs have catered a Musical Feast and have generously contributed some of their special recipes.

Throughout Musical Feasts, *look for* *denoting a chef contributed the recipe.*

John H. Arnold, Beans & Cornbread

Edward Barbieri, Jr., Da Edoardo

Jim Barnett, Unique Restaurant Corporation

Gianni Belsito, Il Posto Ristorante

Jarad Bissel, Duet Restaurant

Tassos Bozadzis, Tassos Epicurean Cuisine

Matt Casadonte, Traffic Jam & Snug

Michael Connery, The Hill Seafood & Chop House

Timothy Giznsky, Opus One

Matthew Kind, The Detroit Club

Karl Kurz, Dakota Inn

Jim Lark, The Lark

Lorraine Platman, Sweet Lorraine's

Jimmy Schmidt, The Rattlesnake Club

Terry Shuster, Fox & Hounds

Marlan Smith, Excalibur

Richard Teeple, Henry Ford Community College

Vienna Coffee Shop

Alan Williams, Brandy's

Takashi Yagihashi, Tribute

Photograph Index

Recipe Index

Recipe Index

Recipe Index

Recipe Index